Grape Leaves

Kahlil Gibran (right) and Mikhail Naimy at Cahoonzie, New York, July 1921.
(Courtesy of Kahlil and Jean Gibran)

Grape Leaves

A Century of Arab-American Poetry

Edited by
Gregory Orfalea and Sharif Elmusa

INTERLINK BOOKS
An imprint of Interlink Publishing Group, Inc.
New York • Northampton

This edition first published 2000 by

INTERLINK BOOKS
An imprint of Interlink Publishing Group, Inc.
99 Seventh Avenue • Brooklyn, New York 11215 and
46 Crosby Street • Northampton, Massachusetts 01060
www.interlinkbooks.com

Copyright © Gregory Orfalea and Sharif Elmusa, 1988, 2000

Originally published by the University of Utah Press

All rights reserved. No part of this publication may be reproduced, stored in a retrieval system, or transmitted in any form or by any means, electronic, mechanical, photocopying, recording or otherwise without the prior permission of the publisher.

Library of Congress Cataloging-in-Publication Data

Grape leaves : a century of Arab American poetry / edited by Gregory Orfalea and Sharif Elmusa.
p. cm.
ISBN 1-56656-338-0
1. American poetry—Arab American authors. 2. American poetry—20th century. 3. Arabic American poetry—20th century—Translations into English. 4. English poetry—Translations from Arabic. 5. Arab Americans—Poetry. I. Orfalea, Gregory, 1949–
II. Elmusa, Sharif, 1947–
PS591.A7G7 1989
811'.008'0892707—dc19

88—19041
CIP

Printed and bound in Canada

PHOTO CREDITS

Ameen Rihani: Courtesy of May Rihani • Kahlil Gibran: Courtesy of Kahlil and Jean Gibran • Mikhail Naimy: Courtesy of Dr. George Selim • Elia Abu Madi (Madey): Courtesy of Robert Madey • Etel Adnan: Simone Fattal • Samuel Hazo: Jonas • Joseph Awad: Don Eiler's Custom Photography • Jack Marshall: Gordon McGregor • Doris Safie: J. Gelfan • Sharif S. Elmusa: B. Lynne Barbee • Lawrence Joseph: Robert Buchta • Gregory Orfalea: Michael Nye • Naomi Shihab Nye: Michael Nye • Elmaz Abinader: Tod Holm

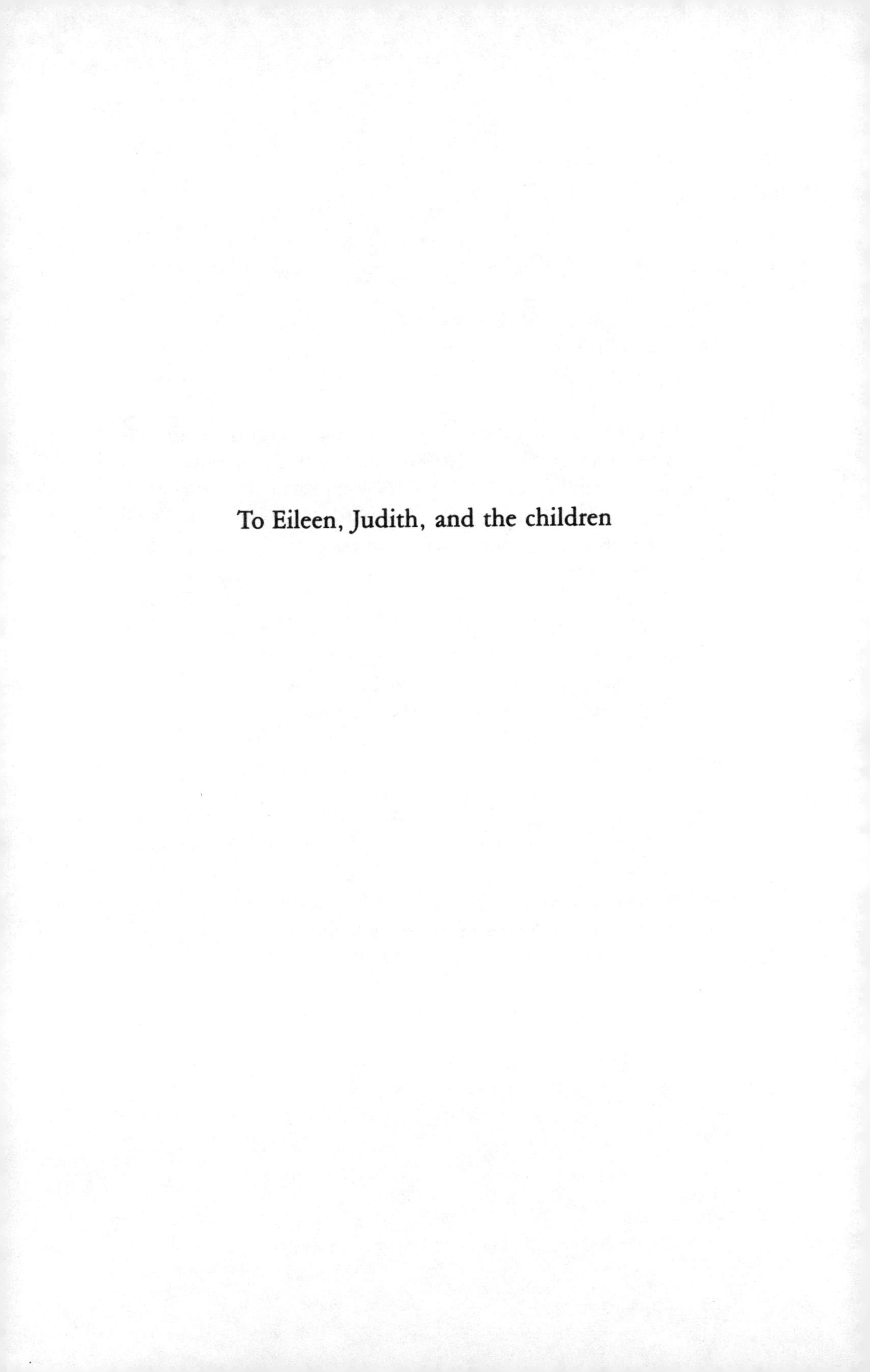

To Eileen, Judith, and the children

Authors' Note

We are delighted that Interlink Publishing is issuing a paperback edition of *Grape Leaves,* whose hardback version, published in 1988 by the University of Utah Press, has long been out-of-print. Our thanks go to Interlink's editor and publisher, Michel Moushabeck, who took the initiative to bring this reprint to light. We feel certain it will answer the many appeals we have heard over the years for copies of this book—at a more reasonable price.

There are several things to note, however, about this 2000 edition. It is, indeed, a nearly exact reprint of the original, with the exception of a new cover, corrections of typographical errors, and resecured reprint rights. Because our new publisher felt it important to produce this *Grape Leaves* paperback in a short span of time, it was not possible to revise biographies or bibliographies of the living writers whose work certainly has grown in the intervening 11 years. Or other interesting facts: for example, Gibran's *The Prophet* continues to break publishing records—there are now 9.5 million copies in print, a 1.5 million increase over the past decade.

We are considering doing a truly updated and expanded anthology of Arab-American writing, which would also feature fiction and creative non-fiction, as well as new work of the poets in *Grape Leaves.* Needless to say, such an edition would have to include selections from poets of real achievement whose work began to be published after the original anthology came out, such as that of David Williams and Khaled Mattawa.

One other correction: the 1988 *Grape Leaves* saluted our wives, Eileen and Judith, for many things, not the least of which were "four beautiful children." In the intervening 11 years, there's been a fifth! So let us name them all here and wish them, too, good reading and eating: Karmah and Layth Elmusa, and Matthew, Andrew, and Luke Orfalea.

GREGORY ORFALEA
SHARIF ELMUSA

Contents

Introduction

When a people leaves the dry, hot lands of civilization's oldest cities (Damascus, Byblos, Jericho) and finds itself in one of the youngest countries on earth—what happens? For one thing, poetry. Like mint in a wall-crack, poetry sprouts from such ruptures of sensibility. It is the purpose of this anthology of poetry by Americans of Arab descent to evidence that fertile rupture.

Arab Americans may be more inclined than most to ask the question: Is it right to isolate a poetry based on ethnic origin? Descended from a people that lived on the crossroads of East and West, their heritage is uniquely international. They know well that poetry is one of the few human means to break through barriers of race, religion, nationality, sex, and language.

When a teacher wants to imbue her black students with a sense of pride, she might read Langston Hughes, Gwendolyn Brooks, or Sterling Brown. There exist poetry anthologies for virtually every American ethnic group: black, Hispanic, Jewish, Indian, Chinese, Armenian, and so on. Until now none has existed for a group whose love of poetry is native and deep: the two million Arab Americans.

Arab American poetry is an especially rich, people-involved, passionate poetry. At the same time, it has been spawned, at least until recently, in isolation from the American mainstream. If art intensifies on peripheries, this is art.

To be sure, the work collected here is accomplished in terms beyond "ethnicity." Included are a former candidate for the Nobel Prize in Literature, a National Book Award nominee, and three recent winners of coveted young poet prizes. In short, *Grape Leaves* is every bit representative of the best in American poetry and its roller-coaster changes throughout the century, as well as, we feel, new nourishment to present at table.

Much of the work of the early Syrian emigré poets is presented in English for the first time to the American public. These writers had to be tough and life-driven. At the turn of the century, the Syrians were considered "next to the Chinese . . . the most foreign of all foreigners" (*Twentieth Century Annual Report of the Associated Charities of Boston*, 1899). Even today, one national columnist called them "the last ethnic group in America safe to hate."

One thing ran in their favor: a belief in poetry that could be traced to the lips of the pre-Islamic tribes; to the poets of Phoenicia, such as Meleager of Tyre; and even back to the Canaanite authors of portions of the *Song of Songs*.

Although forces of modernization are beginning to create the all-too-familiar gulf between poetry and people, anyone who has been to the Middle East has witnessed the remarkable richness of Arab poetry and its direct impact on daily life. Poetry for the Arabs is not isolated in the academy—as too often is the case in the United States—but rather is a public treasure used on important occasions as a connector of people.

For instance, at a funeral in the farming village of Arbeen, Syria, a poet-grandchild of the deceased read a poem as the wood coffin was lowered into the freshly dug grave. The poet—and not the priest or imam—said the last words of farewell, and tears seemed to flow to the inflections of the poem's rhythm. Earlier, at a *haflah*, or evening party, cousins jumped up chanting unplanned poems as salutes to the American travelers and praises to the hoop of the night. There is the Arab tradition of *zajal*, where poets try to outdo each other in extravagant imagery, a kind of poetic duel that serves as popular entertainment.

A James Dickey or Robert Frost reading at a presidential inauguration is a rarity in the United States; for the Arabs, such a conjunction of public ceremony with poetry is practically required. A politician-poet in America (as in the case of Eugene McCarthy) is considered an oddity. In the Arab world, poets engaged in politics, like Nizar Qabbani of Syria, Ghazi Algosaibi of Saudi Arabia, and Palestinian Mahmoud Darweesh, are not uncommon.

Ibn Rashiq, the eleventh-century scholar and critic, put priorities this way: "The ancient Arabs wish one another joy but for three things—the birth of a boy, the coming to light of a poet, and the foaling of a noble mare."

Curiously, contemporary poets of Arab ancestry are less "central" to their communities than they would have been in the old country, or even in the emigré coffeehouses of New York. Among the early *Mahjar* (emigrant poet) Syrians, Kahlil Gibran was the community's unofficial spokesman when Mount Lebanon endured a devastating famine during World War I, cut off by Allied blockades of Turk-held ports. Ameen Rihani was headlined in the *New York Times* during the twenties for debating Jewish spokesmen over the question of Palestine under the British mandate. Perhaps the contemporary poets suffer from the same devaluation of the felt word Ben Bennani notes: "Serious poetry itself occupies a small place in the pop, bang, fast road culture of America."

Nevertheless, during an evening with Arab American poets (five of whom are included here) in 1980, the response was overwhelming. The audience was magnetically attracted to the poets; obviously, the great Arab love of poetry had not been drained from New World veins. In 1982, a pamphlet of twenty pages of such poets' work was published. The enthusiasm was confirmed: *Wrapping the Grapeleaves* went into seven printings totaling fifty thousand copies.

A book-length version, *Grape Leaves*, was the inevitable challenge. A decision was made to connect and present essentially two different eras: that of Gibran's famed New York "Pen League" (*al-Rabitah al-Qalamiyah*), poets who had arrived in America along with millions of immigrants at the turn of the century, and that of the contemporary writers, most of whom write solely in English. It was fascinating to discover elements more vital than ethnicity and U.S. citizenship that these writers share: family; internationalism; metaphysical questioning; homesickness; a marked concern for injustice, violence, and international conflict; a love of gardens and the dance. They also constituted—quite unawares—a kind of internal quarrel with each other. For instance, notice the shifting approach from Rihani's elegy "Gibran" to the debunkings of Gibran by Eugene Paul Nasser ("Disputation with Kahlil Gibran") and Sharif Elmusa ("Dream on the Same Mattress").

With Gibran the anthologist faces a problem the parameters of which can be sensed in these facts alone: he wrote prolifically in both English and Arabic; his early poems in English—some of his best—were "refined" by his benefactress, Mary Haskell; his work appears all over the globe in numerous pirated editions; his Arabic poetry has been subjected to bad editing and translation; he is considered a literary titan by both laymen and literary critics in the Arab world; in America, he is the all-time best-selling author of Alfred A. Knopf, Inc., and at the same time he is virtually ignored, if not actually scorned, by the literati. Strangest of all, excepting appearances of a stray poem in texts, this is the first selection of Gibran's work in a serious anthology of American poetry. Explaining that may lead the reader down the blind alleys of American history as much as into the hallowed corridors of selection which determine just what is "American literature."

We have avoided, we hope, both the excessive adulation and the snobbish dismissal that dominate opinions of Gibran. The extraordinary success of *The Prophet* (eight million copies in print) may be responsible for both. Those whose disregard for Gibran rests on reading only that overwritten, aphoristic book should be encouraged to examine some of the early lyrics such as the powerful "Defeat" and the dramatic monologues from *Jesus the Son of Man*, a fascinating collection of sidelights on Christ by biblical and fictional personae which bears comparision to Browning's *The Ring and the Book*.

Gibran was clearly a revolutionary thinker whose writing was had at much personal sacrifice. If it was prolix, it was serious. America, it appears, supped on Gibran's "fast food" and not on the substantial material, some of which, when translated from Arabic, came with too many "verilys" and "vouchsafes." (We were lucky to receive new translations by Gibran's original translator—Andrew Ghareeb, now in his eighties—of "The Sufi" and the classic "The Gravedigger," the latter a substantial improvement on the Anthony Ferris version in *A Treasury of Kahlil Gibran* and the former written two months before the poet's death and never before published in a collection.)

Though his reputation was built as a love poet, Gibran's literary strength may lie in his social and political material. Some of his best poems are invectives such as "My Countrymen" (unfortunately too long to print here), which blasts the Lebanese (and sectarians in general) as effectively as anything Juvenal aimed at Rome. "Kahlil the

Heretic" is, sadly, as apropros of today's Middle East chaos as it was seventy years ago.

Among the things to keep in mind about Gibran's inflated diction is the fact that it was conditioned by the task he set for himself as a visionary in the Romantic tradition. Whitman, Keats, and Shelley were the poets the emigré Syrians studied in their newfound English, not their actual American contemporaries Eliot, Pound, and Williams. Keats' influence on Gibran he made explicit.

As for Rihani, Mikhail Naimy, and Elia Abu Madi (Madey)—all members of the Pen League—their poetry went virtually unnoticed in their new homeland, though some of it is superior to that of Gibran himself.

Rihani's verse in English tends to be stilted, with forced Victorian couplets (it's curious that he allowed himself to be freer in Arabic, which had no tradition of free verse). The mock heroism doesn't have enough "mock" and is long-winded. Nevertheless, his work written originally in English captures a music—and some arresting thoughts on freedom. No reader will find it difficult to see a conscious, and delightful, imitation of Whitman's "Song of Myself" in the complaint of Khalid, the Bronx peddler.

Naimy's "My Brother" (*Akhi*) deserves comparison to the best antiwar poetry. Like the Englishman Wilfred Owen, Naimy fought in the First World War, though the Lebanese emigré was an American soldier. *Akhi* was never translated into English until 1974 (by Khouri and Algar); ours is a second version. The poem is an unrelenting indictment of mankind for "wanting" the war, but it is filled with pathos. Like Owen, Naimy disagreed with Horace. The new reality of mustard gas and giant war-fronts did not make it "sweet and fitting to die for one's country."

In Naimy we deal with a world-class writer, though he published only one volume of verse, *Hams al-Jufun* (*Eyelid Whisperings*, 1943). His is an obsession with death that borders on the bizarre; it echoes the same obsession Russian poets of the Silver Age had in pre-Bolshevik days. (Naimy himself studied at that time in Poltava, Russia, to be an Orthodox priest, and the stamp of the great Russian novelists and poets of the nineteenth century is upon him.) However, in the stirring "Autumn Leaves" Naimy's reverie finds creation and death moving and, therefore, hopeful. When Naimy exhorts the leaves to "Spread over the earth! / O joy of the eye / ballroom of sun," he has made mortality into a dance. The eerieness of "Rotating Tombs" is worthy of Poe, but its graves, too, have their waltz.

Though a folk hero in the Arab world on the order of a Robert Frost, Elia Abu Madi—unlike the other *Mahjar* poets—did no writing in English, and his wife, who knew no Arabic, never read one of his poems. (She was, incidentally, at age eighty-five eagerly awaiting this volume.) Abu Madi's work is recited by anyone schooled in the Arab world in the past half century. It seems odd that this American should have been so unknown in the land of his choice, especially today in the current rage to translate foreign poets of lesser stature.

Jamil Holway provides a link between the *Mahjar* and the contemporary poets, most of whom were born in the United States. Holway never published a book of poems in Arabic or English, but he was a frequent contributor to Arabic journals in this land, most of which died out as the immigrants had children and grandchildren in whose brains Arabic fluttered and disappeared.

Fifteen of the twenty poets in this collection are living, a number with established or growing reputations. We conducted an ongoing search for lesser-known poets over a five-year-period, finding gems in the corners of old bookstores. Such writers were also brought to our attention, but we established some ground rules: to be considered, the poet had to be a U.S.-citizen of Arab ancestry and had to have published in at least three literary magazines, or at least one book, with work of merit. This necessarily left out some very young voices, and, no doubt, we may have missed a worthy voice or two. Our judgment, of course, is as fallible as the basis of all poetry—the heart. But we found it exhilarating to mix well-known contemporaries, such as Samuel Hazo, with relative unknowns of real caliber, such as Joseph Awad. Quality was our touchstone above all.

Most of these contemporary poets, contrary to the trend, work outside of the academy. They include journalists, lawyers, a corporate executive, an actress, an economist, a civil servant, a storekeeper, a painter. They are Christian, Muslim, Jewish, and Syrian, Lebanese, Palestinian (about 90 percent of Arab Americans originate from the Levant), as well as Moroccan and Iraqi in origin. They have woven into the American tapestry the sand, seas, and streets of concerns sometimes typically American, sometimes not.

Of course, poets have interests peculiar to themselves. For instance, Gibran's obsession with the mad was effected by his Lebanese boyhood proximity to a monastery that housed the insane. Etel Adnan—perhaps influenced by years in San Francisco—offers apocalyptic poetry praising black jazz and Abdul Nasser in Beat fractures. Samuel Hazo's moral distillations contemplate a radio report in a rainstorm, sunken destroyers, and the French and Indian Wars around Pittsburgh. Joseph Awad's religious poems are reminiscent of English metaphysical poetry of the seventeenth century. D.H. Melhem is agonized about gentrification on her beloved New York City's West Side. Lawrence Joseph fumes over a Detroit burned out by race riots in the sixties. Naomi Shihab Nye has produced a wonderful cycle of poems on Latin America, and another important one on the West Bank.

But there are themes that Arab American poets share. They are, in the main, other-oriented. With a major exception, the primacy of family to the poet's selfhood is omnipresent. In fact, one might not be exaggerating to say that for poets of Arab heritage, family *is* self. This is in marked contrast to Emersonian self-reliance because for the Arabs, reliance on the network of family was a key to survival. The sometimes extreme familial closeness has led to poems of a kind of super empathy, where identity blurs. *Rest in Love* by Melhem is a book-length example, a salute to an immigrant mother which ends with a poem *of* that mother, a hymn to Ellis Island.

Tensions between generations are heightened by the unprecedented independence of youth in America, as in "After the Funeral of Assam Hamady," by Sam Hamod. The youthful Hamod describes his embarrassment and awe when his father demands that their streaking car be halted for prayer. The Hajj rolls out his rug—in the middle of South Dakota!—and bows toward Mecca. Touching and hilarious, too, are the "clothespins" of Nasser's Syrian family in the Utica, New York, of the thirties and forties.

"Be a balm when time turns into a speckled snake" says Elia Abu Madi, and it is the wisdom of father speaking to kin. Parental love is in the marvelous series of poems written over twenty years by Hazo about a son born late in marriage. The vitality and undying pull of family is in Bennani's "sad priestess" mother, Marshall's father laying a blanket "beneath the counter every night", and Elmusa's child-to-be, who "breaks my bottle," turning him into "a frightened genie." No father could be more magical than Nye's conjurer of exceptional figs in Dallas.

The family may contain "brother on brother, and shouts" (Orfalea's "My Father Writing Joe Hamrah in a Blackout"); it may conceal paranoia (Joseph's "Sand Nigger"); it may produce little but loss (as in the prayerful mother of miscarriage in Elmaz Abinader's "Making It New"). But family promises the abundance that one's life does not; it promises to overcome time, though the victory may be bittersweet. There is power the gentleness of family ushers into the world, seen in the little boy who rushes into Awad's arms ". . . darkening my vision. / I would die for him. He hangs on tight / As if I might."

The exception to this love of family (at least nuclear and conjugal) is Gibran himself. Gibran did not give a hoot for marriage, either arranged or chosen, that could rule out other "choices." ("The Gravedigger", however, is ambivalent about going it alone.) Like Thoreau, who said marriage would be a foe to his career, Gibran remained single. A Nietzschean freedom was Gibran's idol; it was also his yoke.

It is the human family that is important for Gibran, especially "those whom others defame," and in that he is not alone. The family here is different from the stress on family that sometimes accompanies conservative political and social movements. Without exception, the vision of the poets here extends to embrace the human family, empathize with the underdog, and stand firmly against injustice. The poets do not rest easy in the prevalent isolation of American poetry at large. Descended from a people who have seen so many conquerors (Lebanon alone was sacked by at least seventeen invaders from the Hyksos to the Israelis, not to mention its own self-flagellations), many of the writers seek to bypass nationalism to ferret out the element that unites all humanity—whether it be greed, hope, hatred, or love.

Adnan says, "The divine are the people-who-suffer." Naimy's *Akhi*, directed at the Lebanese, shoots through them to confront mankind with its epitaph for the Great War. Naomi Nye captures something of the reticence and pride of generations of emigrants from the Arab world—and all wanderers: "For you, brothers. For the blood rivers invisibly harbored / . . . confident we are born into a large family / our brothers cover the earth."

Brotherhood has its tragic side, too, shown by Fawaz Turki's touching paean to an Israeli, "In Search of Yacove Eved."

Injustices seen and marked range from near to far. Gibran's "Defeat" was published as a pamphlet and sent to bolster the Serbian rebels at Kossovo in 1918. Abinader holds close to her coal while she spies on the gentry in a Pennsylvania coal-mining town. Suffering at the hands of the powerful galvanizes many of the poets. In fact, the one time the Pen League banded together in a volume was in a special 1916 issue of *al-Funoon* (New York), dedicated to the starving in Lebanon and Syria during the First World War.

It may be said that the best antiwar poetry is written by those who have served in battle, such as Wilfred Owen, James Dickey, and Randall Jarrell. Ex-doughboy Naimy and ex-Marine Hazo are no exceptions. Wars—Korean, Six-Day, Vietnam—come at Hazo from all vantages of his suburban life in Pittsburgh, including what he once termed "the quiet wars" of man and woman.

Yet what does it mean to be of Arab descent? For some of the *Mahjar*, it meant frustration. Rihani, in his Whitmanesque way, laments how poor English inhibits him in talking to women in Central Park: "I can not even like the noon-day bulbul / Whisper with my wings, salaam!" An American enthusiast, Abu Madi once wrote an anthem to the American flag. Naimy was ambivalent about the pulsating land of the free. On the one hand, he compared New York City to a great "Land and Sea Monster"; on the other hand, the atheism of the Soviet Union was not his cup of tea. Clearly, Naimy sought a spirit transformation—influenced by his reading of Lao-Tzu, the Hindus, and Tolstoy—not found in a "shadowland" with its "frenzy to excel." America ultimately was good to Gibran, but one can only wonder at what pain he heard himself laughed off the stage at his reading to the Poetry Society of America. More fundamental blows had already occurred. Within a few years of immigration, and long before he was successful, his mother, sister, and half brother died of tuberculosis in the same year, lost in Boston poverty. He proudly recommended liberty, but the isolation it brought him was abrupt and severe.

As for the contemporary writers, what was lost (or gained) in mixing with America? After removing from the freezer grape leaves that remind him of his dead father, Hamod tries desperately to restudy his Arabic, "though it seems so late." Bennani contrasts the "saffron suns and listless seas" to an American November with "tears and moans at my windowpane." America is variously seen as a place of "cement sentiments," "Columbus' mistake," where "palms stand tall in the smog." But it is also a land where snow falls like "visible love."

An exuberance over the country is often tempered by a kind of bitterness that America has not lived up to its ideals. Hazo identifies with a disillusioned President Wilson after Versailles: "He took no enemy for granted but Americans. / They crippled him." (Ironically, at that very postwar conference Palestinians indicated they preferred an American rather than British or French mandate.)

For Turki, a Palestinian who has taken U.S. citizenship, "Being a Good *Americani*" is a mixture of the quotidian and the pitiable.

Next to family and internationalism, a dogged metaphysical search runs throughout the work of this collection, heightened in the Pen League, but still present in Awad's ruminations, Hazo's quandaries, Adnan's reflections on Mount Tamalpais. Gibran's fascination with the Other (often glimpsed as mad or heretical) is seen throughout—in ghouls, visions, a common enemy, or even a lithe girl slipping barefoot through a rainy gutter (Hazo's "The Drenching"). A spectral vision of Christ comes to Awad as he stares at his father's old barber chair.

The "sacred blur," as William Stafford called it, is often sought through the dance, the perfect accord of body and spirit and motion. It is not surprising to discover that Gibran's last poem was "The Sufi," for it was the Arab and Persian Sufi mystics who whirled in circles while they chanted poetry and praise to God. Rihani's long poem, "A Chant of Mystics"—for all its conspicuous rhymes with "Allahu"—contains an undeniable centrifugal force in its final dimeters.

The dance continues down through the contemporary writers. Doris Safie's "Meditation by the Xerox Machine," brooding on war, seeks "the music of dead / masters, lost in the whirr of the machine." Nye puts a humorous cap on the identity craze:

> When I think of the long history of the self
> on its journey to becoming the whole self, I get tired.
>
> ("The Whole Self")

The poem ends, typically enough for these Sufis of the freeways, with the poet whirling, "leaning headlong into the universe." The self-search is not inward for identity, crystal-hard, but for blurring, merging union with creation, the kind Walt Whitman would have approved, even after the century of misconstrued, self-centered art touched off by his work.

Homesickness in many of the poems is not merely nostalgia. There are conscious efforts (and not so conscious forces) that superimpose ancestors and Arab culture on the present: figs are "emblems," a medal from the Damascus Street of Gold is the gold surf off California, and, finally, the poet. If loss of family means loss of self to the Arab American poet, love can reincarnate the dead in the soul of the living. Hazo makes this clear at the end of "To My Mother," and it is implicit in the shocking immediacy of Hamod's "Lines to My Father."

For immigrants in this collection—whether of the old or new generation—the need to deal with the lost homeland is more urgent than for those born in America. There may be romanticism about Lebanon (Abu Madi), distaste (Gibran), or stoicism over Palestine (Elmusa). Those who suspect the anthology might drain off criticism of contemporary Arab politics should read Turki's "Tel Zaatar Was the Hill of Thyme" and Adnan's "Beirut-Hell Express."

It is interesting to chart the marked involvement of the contemporary generation born in the United States in the conflagrations of the ancestral homeland. In the cases of Abinader, Nye, and Orfalea, concern has been triggered by a number of trips there. In the case of Joseph, it comes from point-blank concentration on the violence meted out on his father's grocery store in Detroit. Detroit-Beirut is the capital city of his work.

Many of the poets address issues as natural for them as it was for Yeats to write about the "terrible beauty" of the Irish rebellion, for Charles Reznikoff to plumb the depths of the Holocaust, or Sterling Brown to sing the trials of blacks in *Southern Road*. But tackling the Arab-Israeli conflicts presents unique pressures to the Arab American writer. There were few Korean-Americans during Korea, few Vietnamese-Americans during Vietnam (immigrants came later, of course). Relatives of both sides of the Mideast conflict have been in the United States for a long time—Jews dating back to the seventeenth century, and Arabs to the middle of the nineteenth century. With the escalation of U.S. arms shipments to Israel since 1967, for an Arab American poet to criticize his country's stance in anything but the most veiled terms was risky. He had no legs to stand on, political or literary, in the halls of power.

To give only one example, after printing an open letter of poets protesting the atrocities in El Salvador, the *American Poetry Review* refused to print a similar missive of poets (many the very same signatories of the previous letter) protesting the Israeli invasion of Lebanon in 1982.

More heartening, Jewish and Arab American poets joined others in a series of readings against the invasion in New York, Washington, D.C., and Detroit, out of which grew the volume *And Not Surrender: American Poets on Lebanon* (Arab American Cultural Foundation, 1982), edited by Kamal Boullata. At least three poems in our anthology here were written in reaction to the 1982 massacres at the Sabra and Shatila refugee camps: "Blood," "The Age of Cruelty," and "The World That Lightning Makes."

Approaches to the Middle East imbroglio are various in theme and technique. Compare Hamod's cinematic "Libyan/Egyptian Acrobats/Israeli Air Circus" with the quietly moving "For Jude's Lebanon" by Awad. Turki is fixated by injustices meted out to Palestinians; Elmusa—who notices the loudspeaker in the minaret—deals with his disenfranchisement stoically. Both grew up in refugee camps, in Beirut and Jericho, respectively. Both now find themselves neighbors in the U.S. capital. It should also be noted that Arab violence against Arab is as grimly apparent to the younger authors as it was to Gibran. The ending of Joseph's "Sand Nigger" is close to despair on this account. Nye asks plaintively after the massacre of Palestinians by Lebanese Christians, "What does a true Arab do now?"

For some, it is to write poetry, which means to not forget. And for the Arab American poet this also means inevitably a relishing of fruits and gardens. They abound in these poems, and a sun both oppressive and life-giving. Greens have always been somewhat miraculous to the Arabs, as if the world were assumed to be more sand than water. (Babylon's Hanging Gardens were a dramatic testimony to that fact.) Tendril-like Arabic calligraphy is also evidence of *horror vacui*, or fear of a void, and in Arab civilization gardens were a primary way of filling that vacuum. Here are grapes, pistachios, mint leaves, apricots, okra (*bamiyah*), and the "gift of Allah"—figs. If one were to point to fruit in these poems, one would have to twist William Carlos Williams into saying, "No ideas but in fruit."

DeRougement has shown in his classic study *Love in the Western World* that romantic love poetry began with a spark from ʿUdhri and Arab Sufi poets, traveled through the medieval French troubadors, and finally reached Byron and Shelley, a trickle drunk by Emerson and a fountain by Whitman. Considering the prevalence of frank sex in contemporary American poetry, there is a curious absence of explicitly sexual poetry among Arab American poets. (Marshall's "The Months of Love" is somewhat of an exception.) This may owe something to the fact that the heightened sensuality of Sufi poetry was rarely explicit, bawdy, or matter-of-fact, though no less erotic. One cannot simply point to strict religious upbringings having patted down candor because of the many examples in literature of the opposite effect. One thinks of that raised Catholic, James Joyce, or the merrily licentious Henry Miller, brought up in a strict Protestant home.

The Middle Eastern family and religions may not inspire as much sexual protestation because of their remarkable combination of firmness and elasticity. More importantly, there is no Augustianian interdiction against sexual passion in Eastern churches such as Antiochian Orthodoxy, as there is in Roman Catholicism. The erotic mysticism of the Hebraic *Song of Songs* relates more readily to Eastern Orthodoxy, with its mystical liturgy and roots, than to mainstream Catholicism. All of this may suggest that the repression that causes blatant sex poetry is not nearly as strong a part of the Middle Eastern religious tradition as it is of that of the West.

It does seem there is more at work than reticence. One of us recalls, for instance, a warning by elders in Los Angeles after having cursed as a boy: *Shu hal-haki*?, or, literally, "What is this talk?" One did not speak the language of the gutter, and the body was holy enough to be spoken of in a poem only in metaphor. Speaking of it as scientific parts was, if not sinful, certainly profane.

Explicit sex reference does not rule out sensuality, which is here in abundance even in matters non-sexual. But one may still ask: Does Arab American poetry gain or lose by a strong streak of Platonism? By its apparent refusal to adopt the "no holds barred" approach of poetry at large in this country? Finally, could poetic Platonism explain the absence from poems by women in this collection of the type of feminist poetry in which the female body is a central theme? The answers are, no doubt, in the making.

Whatever language they adopt, the poets continue, as does Marshall himself, to be "alive / to what / ever eludes closure."

Granting the revolution in Arab poetry effected by the *Mahjar* writers in New York, it is harder to cite what, if anything, contemporary Arab American poets have learned from the complex Arab prosody which, among other things, allows for fifteen figures of speech. *Tibaq*, or oxymoron, occurs in such phrases as Hazo's "the battlefield of any bed" and Joseph's "sun glows gray." Hazo's play with repetition is not unlike that found in the classical Arab *qasida*.

The situational drama common to Arab poetry can be found here, and the love of dialogue in the work of as varied writers as Gibran, Nye, and Hamod. *Jinas* (homonyms in close proximity) can be spotted, and internal rhyming (*tarsi*) seems fundamental to Arab American poetry. A good eye may catch *radd al-^{c}ajz ^{c}ala al-sadr* (ending a line with the same phrase or word that opens it), or *husn al-ta^{c}lil* (ingenuous assignment of cause).

A. J. Arberry, the late Oxford Arabist, said that "rhythm is the most outstanding characteristic of Arabic poetry." There is no doubt that rhythm is endemic to these poems by Arab Americans, from Naimy's dancing leaves to Nasser's "Ooof!" Even the xerox machine is seductively swaying. It is music, these poets seem to say, that coaxes God out of hiding.

Inasmuch as most of the contemporary writers were born here, absorption in modernist American poetics is natural. Free verse is the choice, the dominant mode in the West for this century—though Awad and Hazo have worked fixed forms in a Frostian way. The emphasis William Carlos Williams and Ezra Pound put on the image can be seen in rich imagery—though it tends in Arab American work to be more symbolic than the pure "thing in itself" Imagist doctrine called for. Pound's injunction to "make it new" is taken as an Abinader title. Characteristically, she is not talking solely of poetry, but of children and loss. Elmusa's "stars drizzling" above the refugee camp is as nakedly imagistic as any. Hamod, Adnan, Marshall seem to have been influenced by the wild, unshackled lines and linebreaks of the Beat poets and the projective verse of the Black Mountain writers.

People will not fail to hear the positive negatives, hypothetical narratives, and grime-ridden avowals of another Detroiter, Philip Levine, in the poetry of Lawrence Joseph, though the latter's cadences are uniquely his. A poetry filled with elegy, mostly to family, the collection contains two remarkable literary elegies: one of Awad to Philip Larkin, and one of Marshall to George Oppen. Both demonstrate strong literary kinship with their subjects.

American poetry has never suffered from overpopulation. Arab American poetry contains a number of saints, sinners, uncles, cousins, grocers, inmates, shopkeepers, and garment workers. It is rich with people. The people, in all their foibles, *are* the images, characters developed through action and not objects for exploring the psychoanalytic powers of the poet.

Though Naimy is the most austere of the poets, and acutely aware of the vanity of human wishes, even he suggests acquiescing not just to the earth, but to the earth's "arms." Figures of the human abound in the natural world. And though nature is a force to be respected throughout, as in Adnan's hymn to Mount Tamalpais, and loved, as Nasser listens to an enchanted "plink" of rain on a summer eve, there is really very little of what is an American (Emersonian) genre: nature, or pastoral, poetry. Nature is to be—as in Nye's volcano—negotiated with.

The collection is arranged chronologically by birth of author. A biography is included for each poet, along with a personal statement of purpose—many of them original. Appended notes explain allusions, Arabic words, and interesting contexts.

We asked the living writers in their statements to consider their reasons for writing poetry, conceptions of themselves as Arab Americans and/or the current state of American poetry. Their responses were quite varied and illuminating. With the *Mahjar*, we present as their statements pieces they wrote on the nature of poetry.

Our hope is that the collection will appeal to a wide audience: to Arab Americans, of course, who have long been denied access to this work; to the American literary community; to historians of both the Middle East and the United States; to sociologists; to writers and researchers who must cover the ever-burgeoning miracle of America's ethnic life, as well as the troubled Middle East. Finally, above all, we hope the collection interests anyone who loves a good poem, in Joseph Awad's words, "strongly felt." If that interest spurs the reader on to discover the individual volumes of the poets' work, so much the better.

There are many to thank: first of all, two very special translators, Andrew Ghareeb of Springfield, Massachusetts, and Dr. George Dimitri Selim of Washington, D.C. After being handpicked as a young man by the dying Gibran to translate his first collection into English (*Prose Poems*, 1934), the only translator ever so designated by Gibran, Ghareeb was heartbroken at the poet's death and returned to his hometown of Aitha al-Fakhar, Lebanon. Forty years later, to escape civil war, Ghareeb came back to the United States. We chanced to meet him through his son, Dr. Edmund Ghareeb, a fine historian and critic himself. The elder Ghareeb graciously made available to us a sheaf of other Gibran poetry he had translated in those forty years, as well as "Riddles" by Elia Abu Madi, and work by other members of Gibran's Pen League such as Nasib Arida and Abdul-Messiah Haddad. We only wish we could have printed more.

As for Dr. Selim, he not only gave us pioneering translations of Abu Madi (on whom he did his doctoral dissertation), but, together with his colleague, Dr. George Atiyeh, the director of the Library of Congress Near East section, helped us find old books and articles.

The Immigration History and Research Center of the University of Minnesota afforded the chance to peruse back issues of emigré journals such as *The Syrian World*. Thanks are due to Dr. Rudolf Vecoli and his able staff.

Jean Abinader and Francis Harper, whose Center for Transnational Projects aided us with a generous grant when the manuscript was ready for typing and presentation to publishers, were always enthusiastic supporters. Their friendship is treasured. The workhorse typing chores were performed capably by Neil Narcisso.

We also want to thank the Gibran Kahlil Gibran Education Fund, Inc., in Boston, and its director, Kahlil Gibran (the poet's cousin) for a helpful grant used to defray permission reprint expenses. (This is as good a place as any to recommend *Kahlil Gibran: His Life and Times*, the superb biography of their namesake written by Kahlil

Gibran and his wife, Jean. It is by far the best available book on the subject.)

The University of Utah Press was our guardian angel throughout. The Press' director, David Catron, was a champion from the beginning, Norma Mikkelsen a most congenial and professional editor, and Peggy Lee, the managing editor, meticulous in her inspection.

The poets themselves were ceaseless in their encouragement and generosity for this project, and their cooperation put the lie to the prevalence of poetic turf-battles on the American scene.

We should not forget to thank each other, especially for forbearance when the other was convinced he was right and for the faith to risk disagreement. It is no mean task to co-edit anything, especially when two editors come from such different professional, social, political, and religious backgrounds as we do. Nevertheless, it is our hope that these differences sharpened the selection process, helped us separate the wheat from the chaff. At every point we had to justify to each other opinions each alone might have hardly reconsidered. Our friendship miraculously survives. It was a joyous, and sometimes arduous, tug-of-war.

Finally, the deepest thanks go for the understanding and love of our wives, Eileen and Judith, during a time when we were both unemployed or underemployed and continuing, against reason, to collect this work. Indeed, they graced us during these days not only with their judicious comments on the manuscript and food for the belly, but also four beautiful children.

Gregory Orfalea
Sharif S. Elmusa

AMEEN RIHANI

(1876–1940)

Ameen Rihani

The first American of Arab heritage to devote himself to the writing of literature was Ameen Rihani. Born in Freika, Lebanon, in 1876, he came to the United States in 1888 with his father, a raw silk manufacturer in Lebanon who opened a dry goods store in a lower Manhattan cellar. The store's chief clerk and bookkeeper, the young Rihani cut his new English teeth on bills-of-sale, Hugo, and Shakespeare. Restless, in 1895 he took off with a theatrical troupe for three months, until it sputtered and died in Kansas City, Missouri.

Rihani forged his new roustabout life in turn-of-the-century America into the first—and to date only—novel in English on the Syrian immigrant experience in the United States, *The Book of Khalid*, 1911.

As a poet, Rihani has been credited as the first conscious practitioner of prose poetry in Arab letters. He was also the earliest to translate the blind, brilliant Arab poet of the tenth century, al-Maᶜarri, whose skepticism Rihani found pertinent to modern times. Among his own books of poetry in English are *Myrtle and Myrrh* (1905) and *A Chant of Mystics* (1921). "Gibran" is translated here for the first time from Rihani's collection of prose poetry in Arabic, *Hutaf al-Awdiyah* (*Cry of the Valleys*, 1955).

Perhaps the most politically involved of the early *Mahjar* (emigrant) poets, Rihani shuttled back and forth between the Arab world and the United States, lecturing, carrying the banner of American democracy and Arab independence from Ottoman Turkey and Europe. Permeating his work is the notion of being a bridge between East and West. He wrote numerous articles introducing Arab society to the American reader, published in the *New York Times*, *Harpers*, *Atlantic Monthly*, and the *Nation*. His *The Maker of Modern Arabia* (1928) first chronicled the emergent Saud dynasty in Arabia.

Though he never finished a college degree, Rihani received an honorary doctorate in philosophy from the University of Illinois. Throughout his productive literary life (over two dozen books published, half in English), Rihani was the toast of both the emigrant community and the Arab world, feted at, among other places, the Book Cadillac in Detroit, and at the foot of the Pyramids by a crowd of five thousand guests.

Ever the lover of the American transcendentalists, Rihani consciously imitated Whitman's "Song of Myself" in verse which appears in *The Book of Khalid*, excerpted here under "I dreamt I was a donkey boy again."

After a divorce from his American wife, the artist Bertha Case, Rihani returned to Lebanon and died in Freika in 1940.

"In Loafing"

And Khalid once said to me, "In loafing here, I work as hard as did the masons and hod-carriers who laboured on these pyramids." And I believe him. For is not a book greater than a pyramid? Is not a mosque or a palace better than a tomb? An object is great in proportion to its power of resistance to time and the elements. That is why we think the pyramids are great. But see, the desert is greater than the pyramids, and the sea is greater than the desert, and the heavens are greater than the sea. And yet, there is not in all these that immortal intelligence, that living, palpitating soul, which you find in a great book. A man who conceives and writes a great book, my friend, has done more work than all the helots that laboured on these pyramidal futilities. That is why I find no exaggeration in Khalid's words. For when he loafs, he does so in good earnest. Not like the camel-driver there or the camel, but after the manner of the great thinkers and mystics: like Al-Fared and Jelal[c]ud-Deen Rumy, like Socrates and St. Francis of Assisi, Khalid loafs.

—From *The Book of Khalid*

I DREAMT I WAS A DONKEY BOY AGAIN

I dreamt I was a donkey-boy again.

Out on the sun-swept roads of Baalbek, I tramp behind my burro, trailing my *mulayiah*.

At noon, I pass by a garden redolent of mystic scents and tarry awhile.

Under an orange tree, on the soft green grass, I stretch my limbs.

The daisies, the anemones, and the cyclamens are round me pressing:

The anemone buds hold out to me their precious rubies; the daisies kiss me in the eyes and lips; and the cyclamens shake their powder in my hair.

On the wall, the roses are nodding, smiling; above me the orange blossoms surrender themselves to the wooing breeze; and on yonder rock the salamander sits, complacent and serene.

I take a daisy, and, boy as boys go, question its petals:

Married man or monk, I ask, plucking them off one by one,
And the last petal says, Monk.
I perfume my fingers with crumpled cyclamens, cover my face with the dark-eyed anemones, and fall asleep.
And my burro sleeps beneath the wall, in the shadow of nodding roses.
And the black-birds too are dozing, and the bulbuls flitting by whisper with their wings, "salaam."
Peace and salaam!
The bulbul, the black-bird, the salamander, the burro, and the burro-boy, are to each other shades of noon-day sun:
Happy, loving, generous, and free; –
As happy as each other, and as free.
We do what we please in Nature's realm, go where we please;
No one's offended, no one ever wronged.
No sentinels hath Nature, no police.
But lo, a goblin taller than the tallest poplar, who carries me upon his neck to the Park in far New York.
Here women, light-heeled, heavy-haunched, pace up and down the flags in graceful gait.
My roses these, I cry, and my orange blossoms.
But the goblin placed his hand upon my mouth, and I was dumb.
The cyclamens, the anemones, the daisies, I saw them, but I could not speak to them.
The goblin placed his hand upon my mouth, and I was dumb.
O take me back to my own groves, I cried, or let me speak.
But he threw me off his shoulders in a huff, among the daisies and the cyclamens.
Alone among them, but I could not speak.
He had tied my tongue, the goblin, and left me there alone.
And in front of me, and towards me, and beside me,
Walked Allah's fairest cyclamens and anemones.
I smell them, and the tears flow down my cheeks;
I can not even like the noon-day bulbul
Whisper with my wings, salaam!
I sit me on a bench and weep.
And in my heart I sing
O, let me be a burro-boy again;
O, let me sleep among the cyclamens
Of my own land.

IT WAS ALL FOR HIM

I strolled upon the Brooklyn Bridge one day,
Beneath the storm;
None but a lad in rags upon the way
I saw; – there on a bench he lay
Heedless of form.

He seemingly was reading what the Shower
Was publishing upon the Bridge and down the Bay;
Yet he was writing, writing at this hour, –
Writing in a careless sort of way.

Upon a pad he scribbled and as fast the rain
Retouched, effaced, corrected and revised.
Was he recording Nature's solemn strain,
Or sketching choristers therein disguised?

Whatever it be, I found myself quite by his side:
My nod and smile he pocketed and wrote again;
"Read me your drizzling stuff," I said, and he replied:
"I've written a check in payment for this shower of rain."

From GIBRAN

On the Mediterranean coast, between the estuary and Jubail, I saw three women facing East: one clad in a black dress and a sarcastic smile; another in a white dress, misty-eyed; and yet a third woman adorned with coral, her breast aflame with desire. Three women wailing for Tammuz, asking the dawn, "Did he return? Did he?"

*

From Yahweh's mountains, David's harp replied, and from the meadows of Galilee they heard a voice whisper the name of the Great Nazarene. From the Jordan they heard a voice recite the names of Jeremiah and Isaiah, the son of Amos. In the desert a dove sang, and a folksinger praised the memory of Qais. And from the rostrum of al-Maᶜarri came the words, "Every voice has a field." And like a magnet, Gibran picked the immortal voices scattered in the air, in the history of the East, in letters, and in the scriptures. He heard, he apprehended, and he remembered. He said, "Farewell."

*

In the New World, in the city of iron and heat, amidst the frightful bustle and deafening noise, where the tender are knifed and lofty yearnings are strangled; amidst the overpowering creative current, which enslaves the giants of labor; in the shadow of the skyscraper, which substitutes electricity for sun; in the city of iron and gold, where men live by the watch and the scale, the city which tallies and weighs and measures everything; in New York City lived one who was poor at counting, who revered neither scales nor standards.

*

In the calm of his hermit's house, the dark, light-faced hermit's home, among books and papers, paintings and sculptures, among canvasses over which the quills got weary; among sacramental dolls and cradles over altars, Gibran lived for twenty years. He struggled with the elements that pulled his soul and heart and mind apart, and armed himself with two swords, one from the East and one from the West. He honed the one against what turned rigid in his heart, and polished the other by blending mind and soul. Arabic and English—he struggled with both, and both he kneaded into eloquence. Ten years of sowing and ten years of reaping, ten years brooding and ten contented. With Arabic he triumphed over the mind, with English over the heart.

*

His Arabic flights of mind afforded him refuge from the facts of life, and his English flew him above the fantastic. In both he was a creator: here a lucid word, there a lucid thought.

*

I saw around his throne the three women. The women of Tammuz with the women of New York City, fiction in reality and reality in fiction. I heard them sing, saw them burn incense and leaf through the pages of the immortal book—the book of yearnings and broken wings. I saw the three women around the hearse beseech the blackness of night: "Will he return? Will he?"

—translated by Sharif S. Elmusa

LILATU LAILI

At night on the radiant Rialto,
  By the stars in their houses of glass,
I strolled with my soul in my pocket
  And prayed that my night might not pass;
I have seen 'neath the high heels of Beauty
  My heart and my soul and my shame;
That form! O, how often it lured me,
  And how often I lost in the game!

And how often I walked in the shadow
  Of a Laila a mile and a mile!
But the rapture and bliss of a vision
  Would end in a great gush of bile.
To the hints that her garment would whisper
  I have listened but I would not dare;
I have seen every one of my fancies
  Retreat in the dark of her hair.

I have wished that each building around us
  Was a cedar, a poplar, a pine;
That the men and the women were statues,
  And the rain that was falling was wine;
That the lights were ethereal flowers;
  That the cars were the nooks in the wood,—

* * *

"O, enough!" she exclaimed as she kissed me,
  "This attic and couch are as good."

CONSTANTINOPLE

When Othman's sword, as Paleologue's, is broken
And Othman's gods are smitten to the dust,
And naught remains, not even a rusty token
Of their hierarchal cruelty and lust;
When church and mosque and synagogue shall be,
Despite the bigot's cry, the zealot's prayer,
Unbounded in their bounties all and free
In every heritage divine to share;
When thou shalt rise, rejoicing in thy loss,
Upon the ruins of a state nefast
To reconcile the Crescent and the Cross
And wash thy hands of thine unholy past;
When with the faith new-born of East and West,
Which spans the azure heights of man's desire,
The spirit of thy people, long oppressed,
Is all a-glow with its undying fire;
When thou thyself, Byzantium, shalt stand
In the minaret of Freedom and thy voice,
Rising above the muezzins in the land,
Bids all the seekers of the light rejoice;
When in thy heart the flame of freedom sings,
And in thy hand the touch of freedom glows,
And in thy word the sword of freedom rings,
And in thy deed the seed of freedom grows,

Then shall we call thee Mistress of the Morn,
Bride of the Straits, Queen of the Golden Horn.

From THE FUGITIVE

I ran and still I run away from Thee,
Past pyramids and labyrinths of reason,
Through gleaming forests, where the upas tree
Feeds both the saint and sinner for a season.

And I danced in its lethal shades; I climbed
Up to the highest fruit-concealing bough
That bends beneath a mocking wing; I rhymed
My joy and pride; and o'er the very brow
Of Death I leaped into the howling void,
Where the acrobats of Mind, with balance-pole
Of logic in their hands, are ever employed
In scanning the dark canyons of the Soul.
And I was proud when on the tight rope I
Essayed my feet and fixed my giddy brain
Upon the universe; whereat the sky
Was but a mute infinity of vain
Belief; and every mystery divine,
A sea-washed, iridescent hollow shell
Upon the sands of faith: yea, every sign
Upon the road led to an empty well.
And I was proud—O pride of intellect!—
That the nothingness of things I could detect.

From A CHANT OF MYSTICS

*

Hail, Sana'i, the Moon of the Soul,
The Guide and the Road to the goal.
Hail, Attar, the Vezier of Birds,
Who sing in his musk-scented words.
Hail, Arabi, the Tongue of the Truth,
The Eye of the Prophet, in sooth.
Hail, Rabi^ca, the Heart of the Sphere.
Beloved of the bard and the seer;
The Rosebud that rises to greet
The splendor beneath Allah's feet.
Hail, Gazzali, the Weaver of Light,
The maker of wings for the flight.
Hail, Hallaj, the Diver divine,
Whose pearls decorate every shrine,
Whose blood was the pledge that his words,

I am Truth, shall fore'er be a sign.
To Jelal ᶜud-Din Rumi, all hail!
The Master who flung every veil
To the wind, who ne'er sober was seen,
Though ne'er to the tavern had been;
But ever—and often alone—
Was dancing before Allah's throne.
Hail, Tabrizi, who nourished the Bard
With jasmine and myrtle and nard;—
Who loafed and invited his soul
And would not write a word in his Scroll.
Hail, Fared, the love-stricken one,
The heart of the rhapsodic Sun;
The soul of the Vineyard, the Press
That knew every vineyard's caress:
The host of the Tavern divine—
The Saki, the Cup, and the Wine.

The vision is true,
Allahu, Allahu!
They are garbed in blue,
Allahu, Allahu!
They are drenched with dew,
Allahu, Allahu!

*

Yea, his parrots are we, sugar-chewing
And repeating his words evermore,
While the habitants rude of the world
Camel-like thistles devour.

Sugar-chewing we come for your sake;
Awake, O ye Pilgrims, awake!
The cypress that once graced the grove,
Is a-float on the river of Love.

O Lovers, the Veil of the Secret he rends,
And like light drops of water, he gently descends.

He walks on the face of the turbulent sea,
Driving before him the waves to their lee;
Like a shepherd he calls, and his flock turned to foam,
Scurries and scampers, impatient for home.
A moment, alas! When his face is revealed,
All the wounds of the world are miraculously healed.
A moment, alas! When his light disappears,
The world is submerged in an ocean of tears.

We are the light that is spun
For the firefly and the sun;
We are the thread in the pearls
Of the sea and the tear.

Make use of our pearls, and our foam, and our fire;
For your sake we have come as Disgrace from the sea—

For your sake we have come in the flesh of Desire,
But glory and beauty incarnate are we.
We are the flowers in his Garden, the lights in his Hall.
The sign on his Portal, but he, he is all,—he is all!

The banquet, the host, and the guest—
The seeker, the sought, and the quest—
All three,
Is he.

And we, to rejoin him, like torrents, escape through the hills;
No fetters, no walls can restrain us, no welfare, no ills.

Hope is sighing,
Faith is crying,
Creeds are dying—
Allah, Allah!

A clap of thunder
Rents asunder
Man's little Wonder—
Allah, Allah!

Idols tumble
In a jumble,
Temples crumble—
  Allah, Allah!

Flames are sweeping;
Priests are reaping;
Kings are weeping—
  Allah, Allah!

Ashes cumber
Flame and ember,
Who remember—
  Allah, Allah!

Night is crawling,
Stars are falling,
Souls are calling—
  Allah, Allah!

Orbs are winging,
Fire-bringing,
And of him singing—
  Allah, Allah!

Clove and nard, in
His first garden
Wait his pardon—
  Allah, Allah!

Every flower
In his bower
Is Love's dower—
  Allah, Allah!

His compassion
And his passion
Are our fashion—
  Allah, Allah!

Whirl, whirl, whirl,
Till the world is the size of a pearl.
Dance, dance, dance,
Till the world's like the point of a lance.
Soar, soar, soar,
Till the world is no more.

KAHLIL GIBRAN

(1883–1931)

Kahlil Gibran

Gibran Kahlil Gibran, the legendary author of *The Prophet*, was born in 1883 in Bsharri, a Lebanese mountain village made impassable by snow six months of the year. Though Maronite Catholic, his family held fondly to a story that the poet's mother descended from Muslim converts. At the age of twelve, after leaving a wastrel father, Gibran came with his mother, half brother, and two sisters to Boston. It was there that he would begin a career that launched a revolution in Arab letters from American shores, as well as the career of the young publisher Alfred A. Knopf.

In 1899, the Associated Charities of Boston reported that "next to the Chinese, who can never in any real sense be American, [the Syrians] are the most foreign of all foreigners." Gibran was plucked from Boston's immigrant slums at this time, however, by the top Bostonian literary publisher of the period, Fred Holland Day (Copeland and Day). Day—who published the first poems of Stephen Crane (which Gibran admired at a young age) and introduced Yeats to the American reading public—was a profound influence on young Gibran, whom he took as his protégé. Gibran did illustrations for Copeland and Day books; an accomplished photographer, Day did remarkable studies of Gibran in oriental costume.

Gibran's first writings were in Arabic for small Arabic journals published by emigrés in New York City. His first pamphlet in Arabic, *Music* (1905), was inspired by trips to the Boston Symphony. It wasn't long, however, before his lifelong love and benefactress, Mary Haskell, midwifed Gibran's first halting attempts at English verse into work that made publishing history. *The Prophet* (1923) is the all-time bestseller of Knopf and its parent organization, Random House, with eight million copies in print. All of his eight books in English after several dozen editions still remain in print.

On April 20, 1920, Gibran gathered ten emigré Syrian writers in New York City (among them Rihani, Naimy, and Abu Madi) into "The Pen League" (*al-Rabitah al-Qalamiyah*), in order to lift Arab literature from a quagmire of stagnation and imitation and, as Naimy put it, "infuse a new life into its veins so as to make of it an active force in the building up of the Arab nations." Gibran—having closely studied Walt Whitman—championed free verse and the prose poem, both of which went against the grain of the classical Arab *qasida* and its required monorhyme (each line ending with the same sound). The Pen League changed Arabic literature forever and caused the distinguished critic and anthologizer, Selma

Jayyusi, to call Gibran "the greatest literary figure in Arab letters during the first three decades of this century."

Gibran's success with Knopf propelled him into a circle of titans in America's literary world in the twenties. He published alongside Eugene O'Neill, D. H. Lawrence, Sherwood Anderson, and Robert Frost in the pacifist journal *Seven Arts*. He vied with Edward Arlington Robinson for the attention of Boston poet Josephine Peabody. Though the least of his words would be used at countless weddings, Gibran himself never married.

Like many artists of his day, Gibran was stricken by World War I, and particularly by the famine in Lebanon. A passionate Syrian nationalist, he wrote most of his poems on the subject in Arabic; it was decades before they were translated, oftentimes shoddily. Gibran befriended some who, condemned to death in absentia by the Ottoman Turkish government, had taken refuge in New York.

Gibran's first book with Knopf was *The Madman* (1918). Perhaps his most accomplished in English—reflecting a lifelong fascination with Christ—is the collection of dramatic monologues *Jesus the Son of Man* (1928). Forgotten today is the serious critical praise these two books generated (something that eluded the more lucrative *The Prophet*).

Cirrhosis of the liver and tuberculosis felled Gibran in New York in 1931, where he died in the presence of his best friend, Mikhail Naimy. The poet's body was taken to Bsharri where it lies in a small memorial crypt that has been repeatedly vandalized. Among the many ironies that surrounded his life and death, some of Gibran's endowment to his native village was stolen to buy arms for Lebanon's current civil war, something that would have appalled the poet, who loathed Arab factionalism.

In 1986, the U.S. Congress passed a bill designating a two-acre plot of land across from the Vice-President's residence in Washington, D.C., to be used as a memorial to Kahlil Gibran. For this to take effect, the $1.5 million necessary to construct the site was to be raised by 1989.

In 1991, the Kahlil Gibran Memorial Garden on Massachusetts Avenue was dedicated by President George Bush.

Poets and Poems

If my fellow poets had imagined that the necklaces of verses they composed, and the stanzas whose meters they had strengthened and joined together, would some day become reins to hold back talent, they would have torn up their manuscripts.

If Al-Mutanabbi, the prophet, had prophesied, and Al-Farid, the seer, had foreseen that what they had written would become a source for the barren and a forced guide to our poets of today, they would have poured out their inks in the wells of Oblivion, and broken their quills with the hands of Negligence.

If the spirits of Homer, Virgil, Al-Maary, and Milton had known that poetry would become a lapdog of the rich, they would have forsaken a world in which this could occur.

I grieve to hear the language of the spirits prattled by the tongues of the ignorant. It slays my soul to see the wine of the muses flow over the pens of the pretenders.

Neither am I found alone in the vale of Resentment. Say that I am one of the many who see the frog puffed up to imitate the buffalo.

Poetry, my dear friends, is a sacred incarnation of a smile. Poetry is a sigh that dries the tears. Poetry is a spirit who dwells in the soul, whose nourishment is the heart, whose wine is affection. Poetry that comes not in this form is a false messiah.

Oh spirits of the poets, who watch over us from the heaven of Eternity, we go to the altars you have adorned with the pearls of your thoughts and the gems of your souls because we are oppressed by the clang of steel and the clamor of factories. Therefore our poems are as heavy as freight trains and as annoying as steam whistles.

And you, the real poets, forgive us. We belong in the New World where men run after worldly goods; and poetry, too, is a commodity today, and not a breath of immortality.

—Translated by Anthony Rizcallah Ferris

THE MADMAN (Prologue)

You ask me how I became a madman. It happened thus: One day, long before many gods were born, I woke from a deep sleep and found all my masks were stolen —the seven masks I have fashioned and worn in seven lives —I ran maskless through the crowded streets shouting, "Thieves, thieves, the cursed thieves."

Men and women laughed at me and some ran to their houses in fear of me.

And when I reached the market place, a youth standing on a house-top cried, "He is a madman." I looked up to behold him; the sun kissed my own naked face for the first time. For the first time the sun kissed my own naked face and my soul was inflamed with love for the sun, and I wanted my masks no more. And as if in a trance I cried, "Blessed, blessed are the thieves who stole my masks."

Thus I became a madman.

And I have found both freedom and safety in my madness; the freedom of loneliness and the safety from being understood, for those who understand us enslave something in us.

But let me not be too proud of my safety. Even a Thief in a jail is safe from another thief.

DEFEAT

Defeat, my Defeat, my solitude and my aloofness,
You are dearer to me than a thousand triumphs,
And sweeter to my heart than all world-glory.

Defeat, my Defeat, my self-knowledge and my defiance,
Through you I know that I am yet young and swift of foot
And not to be trapped by withering laurels.
And in you I have found aloneness
And the joy of being shunned and scorned.

Defeat, my Defeat, my shining sword and shield,
In your eyes I have read
That to be enthroned is to be enslaved,
And to be understood is to be levelled down,
And to be grasped is but to reach one's fullness
And like a ripe fruit to fall and be consumed.

Defeat, my Defeat, my bold companion,
You shall hear my songs and my cries and my silences,
And none but you shall speak to me of the beating of wings,
And urging of seas,
And of mountains that burn in the night,
And you alone shall climb my steep and rocky soul.

Defeat, my Defeat, my deathless courage,
You and I shall laugh together with the storm,
And together we shall dig graves for all that die in us,
And we shall stand in the sun with a will,
And we shall be dangerous.

From KHALIL THE HERETIC

From the grasp of Pharaoh
To the claws of Nebuchadnezzar,
To the nails of Alexander,
To the swords of Herod,
To the claws of Nero,
To the fangs of the devil,
Whose yoke is going to enslave us now?
And when shall we fall within the grasp of death
 to find comfort away from the silence of non-existence?

With the strength of our arms they erected the
pillars of their temples and shrines to glorify their gods;
On our backs they brought clay and stones to
build castles to strengthen their strongholds;
And with the power of our bodies they built
pyramids to render their names immortal;
How long are we to build castles and palaces
And live but in huts and caves?
How long are we to fill granaries and stores
And eat nothing but garlic and clover?
How long are we to weave silk and wool
And be clad in tattered cloth?

Through their cunning and treachery they have
set clan against clan;
Have separated group from group;
Have sown the seeds of hate twixt tribe and tribe—
How long are we then to wither like ashes before
this cruel hurricane,
And fight like hungry young lions near this stinking carcass?

In order to secure their power and to rest at heart's ease
they have armed the Durzi to fight the Arab;
Have instigated the Shiʿi against the Sunni;
Have incited the Kurd to slaughter the Bedouin;
Have encouraged the Mohammadan to fight the Christian—
How long is a brother to fight his brother on the
breast of the mother?
How long is a neighbor to threaten his neighbor
near the tomb of the beloved?
How long are the Cross and the Crescent to
remain apart before the eyes of God?

Listen, O Liberty, and harken unto us,
Turn your gaze towards us, O mother of the earth's inhabitants,
For we are not the offspring of your rival;
Speak with the tongue of any one of us
For from one spark the dry straw catches fire;
Awaken with the sound of your wings the spirit
of one of our men

For from one cloud one lightning flash illuminates
valley-lanes and mountain-tops.
Disperse with your resolve these dark clouds;
Descend as a thunderbolt,
Destroy like a catapult
The props of those thrones erected on bones and skulls,
Plated with the gold of taxes and bribery
And soaked in blood and tears.

Listen to us, O Liberty,
Have compassion on us, O Daughter of Athens,
Rescue us, O Sister of Rome,
Save us, O Companion of Moses,
Come to our aid, O beloved of Mohammad,
Teach us, O bride of Jesus,
Strengthen our hearts that we may live;
Or strengthen the arms of our enemies against us
That we may wither, perish and find peace.

—Translated by Suheil B. Bushrui

MARY MAGDALEN

His mouth was like the heart of a pomegranate, and the shadows in His eyes were deep.

And He was gentle, like a man mindful of his own strength.

In my dreams I beheld the kings of the earth standing in awe in His presence.

I would speak of His face, but how shall I?

It was like night without darkness, and like day without the noise of day.

It was a sad face, and it was a joyous face.

And well I remember how once He raised His hand towards the sky, and His parted fingers were like the branches of an elm.

And I remember Him pacing the evening. He was not walking. He Himself was a road above the road; even as a cloud above the earth that would descend to refresh the earth.

But when I stood before Him and spoke to Him, He was a man, and His face was powerful to behold. And He said to me, "What would you, Miriam?"

I did not answer Him, but my wings enfolded my secret, and I was made warm.

And because I could bear His light no more, I turned and walked away, but not in shame. I was only shy, and I would be alone, with His fingers upon the strings of my heart.

A COBBLER IN JERUSALEM

I loved Him not, yet I did not hate Him. I listened to Him not to hear His words but rather the sound of His voice; for His voice pleased me.

All that He said was vague to my mind, but the music thereof was clear to my ear.

Indeed were it not for what others have said to me of His teaching, I should not have known even so much as whether He was with Judea or against it.

MANNUS THE POMPEIIAN TO A GREEK

The Jews, like their neighbors the Phoenicians and the Arabs, will not suffer their gods to rest for a moment upon the wind.

They are over-thoughtful of their deity, and over-observant of one another's prayer and worship and sacrifice.

While we Romans build marble temples to our gods, these people would discuss their god's nature. When we are in ecstasy we sing and dance round the altars of Jupiter and Juno, of Mars and Venus; but they in their rapture wear sackcloth and cover their heads with ashes—and even lament the day that gave them birth.

And Jesus, the man who revealed God as a being of joy, they tortured Him, and then put Him to death.

These people would not be happy with a happy god. They know only the gods of their pain.

Even Jesus' friends and disciples who knew His mirth and heard His laughter, make an image of His sorrow, and they worship that image.

And in such worship they rise not to their deity; they only bring their deity down to themselves.

I believe however that this philosopher, Jesus, who was not unlike Socrates, will have power over His race and mayhap over other races.

For we are all creatures of sadness and of small doubts. And when a man says to us, "Let us be joyous with the gods," we cannot but heed his voice. Strange that the pain of this man has been fashioned into a rite.

These peoples would discover another Adonis, a god slain in the forest, and they would celebrate his slaying. It is a pity they heed not His laughter.

But let us confess, as Roman to Greek. Do even we ourselves hear the laughter of Socrates in the streets of Athens? Is it ever in us to forget the cup of hemlock, even at the theatre of Dionysus?

Do not rather our fathers still stop at the street corners to chat of troubles and to have a happy moment remembering the doleful end of all our great men?

HEAVY-LADEN IS MY SOUL

Heavy-laden is my soul with her own ripe fruit;
Heavy-laden is my soul with her fruit.
Who now will come and eat and be fulfilled?
My soul is overflowing with her wine.
Who now will pour and drink and be cooled of the desert heat?

Would that I were a tree flowerless and fruitless,
For the pain of abundance is more bitter than barrenness,
And the sorrow of the rich from whom no one will take
Is greater than the grief of the beggar to whom none would give.

Would that I were a well, dry and parched,
  and men throwing stones into me;
For this were better and easier to be borne
  than to be a source of living water
When men pass by and will not drink.

Would that I were a reed trodden under foot,
For that were better than to be a lyre of silvery strings
In a house whose lord has no fingers
And whose children are deaf.

THE FOX

A fox looked at his shadow at sunrise and said, "I will have a camel for lunch today." And all morning he went about looking for camels. But at noon he saw his shadow again—and he said, "A mouse will do."

LOVE

They say the jackal and the mole
Drink from the self-same stream
Where the lion comes to drink.

And they say the eagle and the vulture
Dig their beaks into the same carcass,
And are at peace, one with the other,
In the presence of the dead thing.

O love, whose lordly hand
Has bridled my desires,
And raised my hunger and my thirst
To dignity and pride,
Let not the strong in me and the constant
Eat the bread or drink the wine
That tempt my weaker self.
Let me rather starve,
And let my heart parch with thirst,
And let me die and perish,
Ere I stretch my hand
To a cup you did not fill.
Or a bowl you did not bless.

SONG OF THE WAVE

I and the shore are lovers:
The wind unites us and separates us.

I come from beyond the twilight
to merge the silver of my foam with the gold of its sand;

And I cool its burning heart with my moisture.

At dawn's coming I read passion's law to my beloved,

And he draws me to his breast.
At evening I chant the prayer of longing,
And he embraces me.

I am fretful and without rest,
But my loved one is the friend of patience.
Comes the ebb and I embrace my love;
It flows, and I am fallen at his feet.

How I danced around the daughters of the sea
When they rose up from the depths
To sit upon the rocks
And behold the stars!
How I hearkened to the lover
Protesting his passion to a comely maid:
I did help him with sighing and moaning.
How I consorted with the rocks when they were cold and still,
And caressed them, laughing, when they smiled not!
How I delivered bodies from the deep
And brought them to the living!
In what measure did I steal from the depths
Pearls, and gave to the daughters of beauty!

*

In the still night when all created things embrace the phantom
of sleep, I alone am awake, now singing, now sighing.
Alas, wakefulness has destroyed me, but I am a
lover and the truth of Love is awakening.

Behold my life;
As I have lived, so shall I die.

—Translated by H. M. Nahmad

From MY SOUL COUNSELLED ME

My soul spoke unto me and counselled me
to love all that others hate,
And to befriend those whom others defame.
My soul counselled me and revealed unto
me that love dignified not alone the one
who loves, but also the beloved.
Unto that day love was for me a thread of
cobweb between two flowers, close to one another;
But now it has become a halo with neither
beginning nor end,
Encircling all that has been and waxing
eternally to embrace all that shall be.

*

My soul counselled me and taught me to
see beauty veiled by form and colour.
My soul charged me to gaze steadfastly upon all
that is deemed ugly until it appears lovely.
Before my soul had thus charged and counselled me,
I had seemed to see beauty like unto wavering torches
between pillars of smoke;
But now the smoke has dispersed and vanished
and I see naught but the burning.

—Translated by Andrew Ghareeb

DEAD ARE MY PEOPLE

(*Written in exile during the famine in Syria*)

World War I

Gone are my people, but I exist yet,
Lamenting them in my solitude . . .
Dead are my friends, and in their
Death my life is naught but great
Disaster.

The knolls of my country are submerged
By tears and blood, for my people and
My beloved are gone, and I am here
Living as I did when my people and my
Beloved were enjoying life and the
Bounty of life, and when the hills of
My country were blessed and engulfed
By the light of the sun.

My people died from hunger, and he who
Did not perish from starvation was
Butchered with the sword; and I am
Here in this distant land, roaming
Amongst a joyful people who sleep
Upon soft beds, and smile at the days
While the days smile upon them.

*

What can an exiled son do for his
Starving people, and of what value
Unto them is the lamentation of an
Absent poet?

Were I an ear of corn grown in the earth
Of my country, the hungry child would

Pluck me and remove with my kernels
The hand of Death from his soul. Were
I a ripe fruit in the gardens of my
Country, the starving woman would
Gather me and sustain life. Were I
A bird flying in the sky of my country,
My hungry brother would hunt me and
Remove with the flesh of my body the
Shadow of the grave from his body.
But alas! I am not an ear of corn
Grown in the plains of Syria, nor a
Ripe fruit in the valleys of Lebanon;
This is my disaster, and this is my
Mute calamity which brings humiliation
Before my soul and before the phantoms
Of the night . . . This is the painful
Tragedy which tightens my tongue and
Pinions my arms and arrests me usurped
Of power and of will and of action.
This is the curse burned upon my
Forehead before God and man.

And often they say to me,
"The disaster of your country is
Nothing to the calamity of the
World, and the tears and blood shed
By your people are as nothing to
The rivers of blood and tears
Pouring each day and night in the
Valleys and plains of the earth . . . "

Yes, but the death of my people is
A silent accusation; it is a crime
Conceived by the heads of the unseen
Serpents . . . It is a songless and
Sceneless tragedy . . . And if my
People had attacked the despots
And oppressors and died as rebels,
I would have said, "Dying for

Freedom is nobler than living in
The shadow of weak submission, for
He who embraces death with the sword
Of Truth in his hand will eternalize
With the Eternity of Truth, for Life
Is weaker than Death and Death is
Weaker than Truth."

If my nation had partaken in the war
Of all nations and had died in the
Field of battle, I would say that
The raging tempest had broken with
Its might the green branches; and
Strong death under the canopy of
The tempest is nobler than slow
Perishment in the arms of senility.
But there was no rescue from the
Closing jaws . . . My people dropped
And wept with the crying angels.

If an earthquake had torn my
Country asunder and the earth had
Engulfed my people into its bosom,
I would have said, "A great and
Mysterious law has been moved by
The will of divine force, and it
Would be pure madness if we frail
Mortals endeavoured to probe its
Deep secrets . . . "
But my people did not die as rebels;
They were not killed in the field
Of battle; nor did the earthquake
Shatter my country and subdue them.
Death was their only rescuer, and
Starvation their only spoils.

*

My people and your people, my Syrian
Brother, are dead . . . What can be

Done for those who are dying? Our
Lamentations will not satisfy their
Hunger, and our tears will not quench
Their thirst; what can we do to save
Them from between the iron paws of
Hunger? My brother, the kindness
Which compels you to give a part of
Your life to any human who is in the
Shadow of losing his life is the only
Virtue which makes you worthy of the
Light of day and the peace of the
Night . . . Remember, my brother,
That the coin which you drop into
The withered hand stretching toward
you is the only golden chain that
Binds your rich heart to the
Loving heart of God . . .

—Translated by Anthony Rizcallah Ferris

THE SUFI

To God the praise be,
Neither gold nor silver
Have we.
No movable
And immovable property.
Yoke-companion none.
Nor offspring.
And without lineage.
Through the earth
Which stretches wide,
As a phantom we traverse
Whom no one can perceive
Save in whose twin orbs
The phantom hides.
If we laugh,

Distress lurks in Time,
And if we weep
Behind it joy lies.
We are but a spirit!
Should you say to us:
"How wondrous!"
Then forthright we reply:
"By heaven!
Wonder dwells
In your own
Veil of clay."

—Translated by Andrew Ghareeb

THE TWO POEMS

Many centuries ago, on a road to Athens, two poets met, and they were glad to see one another.

And one poet asked the other saying, "What have you composed of late, and how goes it with your lyre?"

And the other poet answered and said with pride, "I have but now finished the greatest of my poems, perchance the greatest poem yet written in Greek. It is an invocation to Zeus the Supreme."

Then he took from beneath his cloak a parchment, saying, "Here, behold, I have it with me, and I would fain read it to you. Come, let us sit in the shade of that white cypress."

And the poet read his poem. And it was a long poem.

And the other poet said in kindliness, "This is a great poem. It will live through the ages, and in it you shall be glorified."

And the first poet said calmly, "And what have you been writing these late days?"

And the other answered, "I have written but little. Only eight lines in remembrance of a child playing in a garden." And he recited the lines.

The first poet said, "Not so bad; not so bad."

And they parted.

And now after two thousand years the eight lines of the one poet are read in every tongue, and are loved and cherished.

And though the other poem has indeed come down through the ages in libraries and in the cells of scholars, and though it is remembered, it is neither loved nor read.

THE GRAVEDIGGER

In the valley of the shade of life
Strewn with skulls and bones,
Solitary I walked
During a night whose mist
Concealed the stars
And awe commingled with silence.
Upon the river banks
Of blood and tears,
Gliding as a spotted serpent
And stirring as the criminals' dreams,
Listening I stood
To the whispers of shadows
And gazed fixedly at nothing.
When the night was half-spent,
A procession of demons
Leaped from their pits.
Heavy-falling steps
I heard drawing toward me,
I turned, and lo,
A giant shadow
Was standing before me.

Terror-stricken I shouted,
"What would you of me?"
Then with eyes gleaming like lamps,
He looked at me
And calmly said,
"Nothing would I of you
Yet, everything."
I said,
"Solitude I came seeking.
Let me be
And wend your way."
Smiling, he said,
"My way is but your way,
For where you go I go,
And stay where you stay."
Then I said,
"Seeking solitude came I;
Thus to my solitude leave me."
He answered saying,
"Solitude itself am I.
Why you are afraid of me?"
I replied,
"I am not in fear of you."
Then said he,
"If you are not afraid of me,
Why are you shaking
Like a reed before the wind?"
I said,
"The wind is playing sport
With my garments."
Then with a burst of laughter,
A roaring tempest,
He retorted,
"You are but a coward
Afraid to be afraid of me.
Thus your fear is two-fold.
But you are trying to hide it from me,
A deceit
Weaker than the spider's webs.

You make me laugh!
And you anger me."
On a huge rock,
With him I sat
In spite of myself.
After what seemed a thousand years,
Scornfully he looked at me
Then asked;
"What is your name?"
"My name is Abdullah."
Then he said,
"Indeed numerous are the slaves of God,
And great are the wearies of God
of His slaves.
Why not call yourself
The master of demons
And hereby add to their load of evil?"
Said I,
"My name is Abdullah,
And a dear name it is,
That my father gave me."
Said he,
"The fathers' gifts
Are but the children's curse,
And unless one be rid
Of his fathers and forefathers' gifts,
He remains a slave of the dead."
I bowed my head,
Contemplating his words.
Then he renewed,
"What is your trade?"
"Verses of poetry I scan
And to sounding prose I turn them.
Also I have opinions of life,
Which I exchange with the people."
He said,
"This is an ancient
And forsaken trade—
Neither helps nor hurts them."

"What shall I do
With my days and nights
To help and benefit the people?"
He answered,
"Adopt for yourself
The trade of gravedigging,
Thus you will be relieving
The living from the dead bodies
Which lay heaped about their dwellings,
Their courts of justice
And their places of worship."
I said I had never seen dead corpses like that.
He said,
"You perceive with your misconstrued eye only,
For you see the people
Trembling before the tempest of life,
Deeming them alive
While living-dead they are
Ever since they were born,
Finding no one to bury them.
So they remain prostrate
Above the surface of the earth,
While the smell
Of their offensive stench
Comes forth."
I replied, in fear,
"How am I to distinguish
Between the living and the living-dead,
When both tremble before the tempest?"
He said,
"The living-dead indeed shakes
Before the tempest,
But the living runs along with it,
And doesn't stop until it stops."
Then he reclined against his arm,
And his cord-twisted sinews
Appeared like the roots
Of an oak-tree
Full of vigor and life.

"Are you married?"
"Yes," I replied,
"My wife is a beautiful woman,
And I am fond of her."
"How great are your faults
For marriage is man's bondage
To custom and habit,
But if you wish to be free,
Then divorce your wife."
"Three sons have I,
The eldest still plays with balls
And sports with marbles,
And the youngest ruminates words
But cannot speak them.
What shall I do with them?"
He said,
"Digging graves teach them.
Give each one a spade
And let them be."
I replied,
"I cannot brook to be alone,
For I became accustomed
To the enjoyment of life
Among my wife and my little ones.
If I leave them,
Happiness will leave me."
He said,
"Man's life amongst his wife
And his children
Is but a black wretchedness
Hidden behind white darkness.
But if you must be married,
Take in wedlock
A maiden of the daughters of the djinns."
Finding this strange, I said
"There is no reality to the djinns.
Why are you deluding me?"
Then he said,
"What an unintelligent fellow you are!

For there is no reality
To anyone but the djinns,
And he who is not of the djinns,
Finds himself living in a world of suspicion
And of confusion."
Then I asked,
"Have the daughters of the djinns
Grace and beauty?"
He answered,
"Theirs is a grace
That will not perish,
And a beauty
That doesn't wither or fade."
"Show me but one djinniyah
And convinced I will be."
"Were it possible for you
to behold and touch a djinniyah,
I would not have admonished you
To marry her."
"What good or benefit is a wife,
Neither seen nor touched?"
Forthright he said,
"It is a slow benefit,
Such as the extinction of the creatures
And the vanishing of the dead
Who shake before the storm
And don't walk along with it."
He averted his face from me.
"What is your faith?"
I replied,
"I believe in God
And honor His prophets.
I also love virtue
And have great hope in life to come."
He said,
"These are only passages,
Which the bygone ages set down
And quotation put them
On your lips by habit.

But the real truth is
That you believe
Only in yourself,
Love not other than it
And its inclinations,
And you have no hope
Save in its immortality.
For since the beginning
Man worshipped himself,
Calling it by different names.
Which vary with his hopes
And inclinations.
Now he names it: Baal,
Now: Jupiter,
And another: God."
He laughed and continued,
"But how strange are those,
Who worship themselves,
While stinking corpses
They are themselves."
I shouted,
"If you have a master,
By your Heaven tell me who you are!"
He replied,
"My own master am I."
"What is your name?"
"The Mad."
"Where were you born?"
"Everywhere."
"When were you born?"
"In all times and periods."
"Where learned your wisdom,
Who disclosed to you life's secret
And revealed to you
The mysteries of existence?"
He replied,
"I am not a wiseman,
For wisdom is an attribute
Of the weakly human beings.

But I am a strong madman.
I walk and the earth reels
Under my feet.
I stop and the procession of stars
Stops with me.
And I learned to mock mankind
From the demons,
Understood the mysteries
Of being and nonbeing
After associating
With the kings of the djinns
And accompanied the giants of nights."
I asked,
"What are you doing
In these rugged valleys?
How do you spend your days
And nights?"
He answered,
"In the morning
I blaspheme the sun.
At noon I invoke evil
Against men.
Evening nature I ridicule.
And at night,
Before myself I kneel
And worship.
Time, the sea and I—
We sleep not at all.
But we devour the bodies
Of men
And absorb their blood
And find their gasps
Gently pleasing."
Then he stood up,
Buckling his arms to his breast,
Looked straight at my eyes
And with deep and quiet voice,
He said,
"Adieu, for I go

Where the giants and the ghouls meet."
I shouted,
"I have another question
To ask!"
He answered,
While part of his form
Was hidden
In the hung mist of the night,
"The mad gods
Grant respite to no one;
Therefore, fare you well,
Till we meet,"
Disappearing from sight
Behind a curtain of darkness.
His voice rippled
Amid the lofty rocks,
"Adieu, till we meet, till we meet."
The following day,
I divorced my wife
And took in wedlock
A daughter of the djinns,
Then gave each of my sons
A pick and a spade
And told them,
"Go, and whenever you see a dead man,
Bury him."
And ever since that day
Until now
Graves I have been digging
And interring the living-dead.
But many are the dead,
While I am alone
With no one to assist me.

—Translated by Andrew Ghareeb

JAMIL HOLWAY

(1883–1946)

Jamil B. Holway

Jamil B. Holway (1883–1946), born and educated in Damascus, Syria, graduated from the American University of Beirut. Early in the century he settled in Chicago, where his parents were already living. Later he lived in the South (Missouri, Texas, Louisiana, and Tennessee). In 1907 he was appointed by the U.S. Federal Government as an interpreter and examiner in the Immigration Service. In 1918 he resigned his job to practice law. In 1928 he moved with his family to Brooklyn, New York, where he resided for the remainder of his life. During the Second World War, Holway worked in the "Fight for Freedom" drive for the U.S. Office of War Information.

Holway's contributions to Arab American newspapers and magazines brought him admiration and recognition. Although *al-Muhajir al-Suri* (The Syrian Immigrant), which appeared in New York in 1910, is his only published book, Holway's scattered poems and essays provide us with an interesting glimpse of a poet who wrote at Gibran's time, but outside of his immediate circle.

"Strip Every Nation"

Poetry is the widest, most wonderful, most comprehensive and effective means to convey knowledge and feeling because it touches the heart and penetrates the soul; then it goes to the mind, striking it with a magic wand, even though it may be made of stone.

With the discovery of poetry and poetic writing, man has discovered the beauty of his essence and his high position among creatures. In my opinion, the first to discover this beautiful art deserves to be honored more than the greatest discoverer or inventor, and more than the most sensible professional or industrialist.

The greatness of every nation stands on its men; and the men of the nation are poets, writers, politicians, inventors, those who excel in their crafts, financiers, and clergymen. And to me, the best, the most honorable, and the most knowledgeable of them all are the poets and writers. Strip every nation of its poets and writers, and you will see how much its honor and rank diminish.

—Translated by George Dimitri Selim

SATAN

Satan came to me in my dream
desirous to dispute with me.
With his frightful horns and flaming eyes
he got close to me.
"Go away!" I said, "Beat it, damn you!
Don't disturb my thoughts."

"I came to entertain you," he said,
"with my knowledge, skill, and experience.
Answer me! Who are you?"

"One of the sages of the earth," I said,
"Or haven't you heard of my fame?
I have filled the world with poetry
Won't you softly murmur my poems in hell?"

He burst out laughing
at my talk in surprise and scorn.
"Is there hope for wisdom on earth,
or for goodness from its evil people?
If people were just
they would exalt my value in their hearts.
When God created them,
He knew that they would disobey Him forever.
He built them hell,
and chose me to punish them and take revenge.
It's because of them that He threw me in the abyss,
and I lost my might, authority, and power.
Between them and my Lord I was the victim.
Woe unto them!
The fire of hell did not frighten them,
nor did they learn from my fall.
They persisted in their doom,
disturbing God's peace and mine,
and my patience.
Since they erected hell among themselves
my home is vacant of devils.
They all reside in people's souls,
striving for evil and harm.
Don't you see them
making servants of fuel and wind,
flying in space like birds,
hurling fire at mankind,
heedless of harm and destruction?
Don't you see them on earth
surging and agitated like lions and leopards?
Don't you see them
making the whales captives,
causing death to rage,
and the interior of the seas to tremble?
How could Moses think
that the Lord created man
—from the very beginning—in His image?
I die of shame
when they say that they are my followers."

In the intensity of my anger
I struck Satan for despising men.
But when I woke up
and my eyes wandered over the newspaper,
and saw life a torrent of fire
in a hell of horrors and dangers, I said:
"Contentious though they might be
Satan's words are true."

—Translated by George Dimitri Selim

THROBBINGS

Zaynab complained against me
to the judge of love.
"He has sly eyes," she told him,
which roam around me
to devour my beauty.
Judge of love!
I am not safe anymore.

"I think his eyes are two bees
raiding the honey
which sweetens my lips.
I see them as two eagles
hovering in space.
descending to snatch me.
I think, and from my fear,
I think strange things.
God knows how much I suffer from my thoughts.

"He invaded me with his eyes
and, as if this were not enough,
he tried to lower my standing among people.
Hypocritically, he said
that I have stolen my beauty from the universe,
and that it was not created naturally in me.
That I have plundered the morning for a face,

the dusk for hair,
uniting both in me.
That from the gardens
I have stolen the flowers for cheeks
—my cheeks are rosy.
That I have covered my neck with pure snow,
and that my eyes are tinted with narcissus.

"When my voice enchanted him
he denied it, and said:
'It's a nightingale singing in the garden.'
With sword-like glances I struck him,
he said, and in his deep-red blood
I dyed my finger tips
and in his poems he chanted alluding to me.
So people said:
'His meanings are necklaces of pearls.'
Lord of verdicts!
Administer your justice between us.
Enough of his straying in love.
I've had enough!"

When the time of complaint was over,
the judge asked me:
"What is your answer.
you who are so passionately in love?"
I said:
"I find . . . that I am a criminal.
My insanity may not be deferred.
She has dispossessed me
of mind and heart."

—Translated by George Dimitri Selim

MIKHAIL NAIMY

(1889–1988)

Mikhail Naimy

Until very recently, the only surviving poet of Gibran's circle in New York City lived in the town of his birth, Baskinta, high in the Lebanese mountains. Mikhail Naimy (in Arabic, Nu'aymah) died in 1988 at age ninety-nine. He was probably the most acclaimed writer in the Arab world and was considered for the Nobel Prize in Literature. To his fellow Americans, however, Naimy is virtually unknown. Naimy lived here twenty years and wrote most of his poetry in the United States. He also served with the U.S. Army in World War I. From his experience on the French front came the renowned war poem "My Brother," or *Akhi*.

Naimy's life spanned the countries of the great powers. He studied for the Orthodox priesthood in Poltava, Russia, abandoned the seminarian's robes after an agonized love affair with a married woman, came to the United States in 1911, and received a law degree from the University of Washington, Seattle. It was from the Northwest that he wrote a shrewd criticism of Gibran's novel *The Broken Wings*. It elicited an invitation from Gibran to come to New York City.

Naimy became the critical driving force of the Pen League, declaring "all-out war on hypocrisy in literature" in his landmark critical work, *The Sieve* (*al-Ghirbal*). But when Gibran died in 1931, Naimy left the United States and finished *Gibran Kahlil Gibran*, a biography of his famous friend, in Lebanon.

Long after individual poems became part of Arabic literature textbooks, Naimy's poetry—most of it written during New York days—was collected in one book, *Eyelid Whisperings* (*Hams al-Jufun*, 1943), which has not been published in English. His work trades romantic vehemence for a poetry so strange yet peaceful in its dark stoicism that one critic called it "poetry *a mi-voix*" (poetry of quiet voice). "Rotating Tombs" and "The Cord of Hope" are translated here for the first time in English.

As with Rihani and Gibran, but to a lesser extent, Naimy experimented with writing poetry in his newfound English. Three of these poems found their way onto the editorial pages of the *New York Times* just before and at the onset of the Great Depression (of those "A Solemn Vow" and "Hunger" are here). The fever of American competitiveness clearly bothered Naimy, and the pleasures of the Roaring Twenties did not faze this man of sublime denials. In "The Endless Race" he exhorts a friend to "stride along unmindful of the jeers / Or cheers of those who loiter on the road."

Naimy published a Nietzschean verse drama about a spiritual search, *The Book of Mirdad* (1948). But he was most prolific in fiction. One critic calls his "the first mature attempt to create the really Arabic short story," with a flavor of Chekhovian realism. Many of the stories in the untranslated *Kana ma Kan* (*Once Upon a Time*, 1937) are set in and inspired by the Syrian enclave in which Naimy lived in New York City. *Memoirs of a Vagrant Soul* (or Pitted Face), translated into English in 1952, is a searing novel of a guilt-possessed young man who murders his wife on their wedding night. *Memoirs*, also set in New York City, has been compared in its power to the work of Dostoevsky.

At the age of forty-three, Naimy took a vow of chastity and devoted himself to asceticism and the examples of Buddha, Lao-Tzu, Christ, and al-Hallaj. In 1957 he published *Beyond Moscow and Washington*, a book that posited a "third way" of spiritual and community life before the phrase "Third World" had currency. Excepting his years in America, for a good part of the twentieth century Naimy—the "Old Man of the Mountain"—lived in Baskinta and saw the world through a ravine named the Valley of Skulls, communing beyond the stars and stripes and probably beyond the cedars.

From *al-Sabun (At Seventy)*

*I expended no little effort to drive this poison out of my system—the poison of brazenly hypocritical lip-service that, with a perfectly straight face, says other than its inward thoughts and thinks inwardly other than what it says. This was my prime concern when I first began to write—to declare all-out war on hypocrisy in literature, and to insist above all on honesty and sincerity in all our verse and prose, before metrical resonance or brilliance of diction or succinctness of expression. In my very first article [*The Sieve*] I raised the cry:*

> *Sincerity! . . . if only we had so much as a mustardseed! The very word has become as distasteful to us as, say, "dung-beetle"; the virtue it refers to no longer has any place in a life moulded by deceit, hypocrisy, flattery and vainglory.*

Perhaps even at that tender age I had some inkling of this, though I could not have put it into words. How else to account for my early inclination towards seclusion and silence, so much that one of my aunts used to call me "the Silent Lady"? She was surprised that I did not raise a din, get into fights and let myself go during play like other boys. In fact I hated uproar, scuffling and quarrelling. When I did play, I was gripped by the enthusiasm of the game—but only for a time; soon I would leave the arena and go off in search of a quiet spot on the bank of a stream or in the shade of a pine, where I would become engrossed by the activities of a scarab beetle rolling a ball of dirt, an ant dragging along a single seed, a sparrow searching for an insect, or a small cloud scurrying across the vast blue firmament above my head. Or in drawing enigmatic lines and shapes in the sand in front of me. And often in these moments of solitude there would creep upon me the feeling that I was not alone. Often, too, I would talk with these people I fancied were with me, though not aloud.

—Translated by J. R. Perry

From THE CORD OF HOPE

Hope is agony,
yet we hope.

We hope secretly
while hope publicly mocks us.

Even denying hope,
I hope. And I resent it.

Hope is the whip of Time
spurring us forward.

And I seek to be a sage when young,
to recover youth's paradise when old,

to be free by virtue of that illness, love,
and a captive of love when I'm free,

to be eloquent when reticent
and reticent when pearls come in my speech.

We all sow hope.
And after all our toil, hope is all we reap.

Hope is a tightrope
on which we teeter above the sea of life
like acrobats.

Yet hope nibbles its own cord
as the seconds eat away their thread.

—Translated by Sharif S. Elmusa
with Gregory Orfalea

MY BROTHER

Brother, if on the heels of war Western man
celebrates his deeds,
Consecrates the memory of the fallen
and builds monuments for heroes,
Do not yourself sing for the victors nor rejoice
over those trampled by victorious wheels;
Rather kneel as I do, wounded, for the end of our dead.

Brother, if after the war a soldier comes home
And throws his tired body into the arms of friends,
Do not hope on your return for friends.
Hunger struck down all to whom we might whisper our pain.

Brother, if the farmer returns to till his land,
And after long exile rebuilds a shack
which cannon had wrecked,
Our waterwheels have dried up
And the foes have left no seedling except the scattered corpses.

Brother, misery nestled everywhere—through our will.
Do not lament. Others do not hear our woe.
Instead follow me with a pick and spade that we may
dig a trench in which to hide our dead.

Dear brother, who are we without a neighbor, kin or country?
We sleep and we wake clad in shame.

The world breathes our stench, as it did that of the dead.
Bring the spade and follow me—dig another trench
for those still alive.

—Translated by Sharif S. Elmusa
with Gregory Orfalea

AUTUMN LEAVES

Spread over the earth!
O joy of the eye
ballroom of sun, O
swing of the moon
O organ of night and O
guitar of dawn!
Sign of the restless,
art of the wayward,
memory's total glory—
the trees have cast you off.

Dress our earth!
Touch, leaf to leaf,
the shadows of the lost,
then raise your head to the vast blue:
the past will not return.

And once you leave old friends behind
dance your heart to the caravan
of Fate. Touch, leaf to leaf.
Cast no blame on branch, wind, or cloud.
They cannot soothe; they cannot reply.

Time is ripe with wonders
spreads a wake of ruins
stills desire, and does not heed a plea.
Go on—blame no one—

back to the arms of the earth.
Turn the Wheel once more.
Forget your faded beauty:
the past will not return.

How many roses before you bloomed
and how many did fade!

Do not be afraid; Fate is not at fault.
The jewel we have lost
we will find again in the grave.

Go back to the arms of the earth.

—Translated by Sharif S. Elmusa
with Gregory Orfalea

A SOLEMN VOW

(*To One Who Worries Overmuch*)

Have peace, O restless, sorrow-laden heart!
I shall not laugh
Until with sorrow I have made you part
As parts the wheat, when winnowed, from the chaff.
Till then I shall not laugh.

O sleepless eyes that weep, yet shed no tears,
I shall not sleep
Until from you I've banished cares and fears
That dimmed your light and taught you how to weep.
Till then I shall not sleep.

O spirit once athrob with song, now mute,
I shall not sing
Until once more I've made you like a lute
Attuned to quiver in Love's hands and ring.
Till then I shall not sing.

O God's fair image, lost in Shadowland,
I shall not die
Until I've torn your veils and made you stand
A naked loveliness beneath the sky.
But then—I will not die.

HUNGER

Into my heart a seed was cast
And it took root and sprouted fast.

It spread so far and reached so high,
Until it filled the earth and sky.

And now its boughs are weighted low
With fairer fruit than angels know;

Yet I whose heart sap feeds the root,
Though famished, dare not eat the fruit.

CLOSE YOUR EYES AND SEE

When clouds conceal your skies,
Close your eyes;
And see the stars beyond.
If earth is wrapped in snow,
Close your eyes;
And see the flowers below.
When sickness knows no ease,
Close your eyes;
And see the cure in the disease.
And when the tomb gapes wide,
Close your eyes;
And see the cradle there inside.

—Translated by J. R. Perry

ROTATING TOMBS

Come, love, hail the tombs,
sip the nectar of Time,
and if we see the bones
spring into roses
we know that life is rotating tombs.

Come. Leave hope behind and stretch
your sight to the zenith.
You'll see the sun moves by Fate
and know that to live is to give in.
Hope? A twinge of living.

Come. Forsake the struggle
of good and evil.
If you whisper in dawn's ear
and dusk answers back
you'll wonder: is dusk the brother
of dawn, evil the brother of good?

Pretend you forget your youth.
Drive the wind through an army of clouds.
Is cloud-water young or old?
Isn't youth, isn't age, a cloud
and we a cloud's tears?

Leave truth to liars
and clean love to lovers
and dignity to hoarders of gold
and knowledge to the witless
and all your night trials
and the frenzy to excel leave to the beggar.

Your eyes shine their light
over the mocking ruins
that stare back with Time's undeceiving eyes
at the sand in your eyesockets
and the worm behind the eyelids.

Beauty? Pass by if vain and unseen
by Time. Abandon war and ambition,
abandon palaces. Hail the tombs!
Generations wheel over the world.
Aren't we all rotating tombs?

—Translated by Sharif S. Elmusa
with Gregory Orfalea

ELIA ABU MADI (MADEY)

(1890–1957)

Elia Abu Madi (Madey)

Perhaps the least known of the *Mahjar* writers—because he wrote only in Arabic and has rarely been translated—is Elia Abu Madi (Madey). However, Abu Madi was considered by Gibran and his fellows to be the cream of their New York group. Indeed, Abu Madi's four poetic volumes of skepticism and hope contain work memorized by students throughout the Arab world. Yet Abu Madi, unlike Naimy and Rihani, never returned to stay in Lebanon and lived most of his adult life in the United States. He was a fervent American patriot, who once wrote a hymn to the flag which sang out, "On it the stripes escort the stars / True shelter is under it / Long live America, the best sanctuary / From generation to generation!" Abu Madi enjoyed playing whist with his fellow immigrants and even tried his hand at golf.

Born in 1890 in al-Mahaydatah, Lebanon, Elia Abu Madi was educated in Cairo, where his first book of poems, *Diwan Tidkar al-Madi* (*Remembrance of the Past*), was published in 1911. However, the Ottoman authorities felt his writings were too provocative and Madey was forced into exile in 1912, living awhile in Cincinnati before coming to New York City in 1916.

Abu Madi met and married Dora Diab, whose father had been editor of the first Arabic newspaper in America, *Kowkab America*, and later *Mirat al-Gharb* (*Light of the West*). Abu Madi himself took over *Mirat al-Gharb* at his father-in-law's death, and later began his own newspaper, *Al-Samir*, published five times a week until his own death in 1957 in Brooklyn. Dora and Elia had three sons; one of them worked on the Apollo mission for NASA, and another was chairman of the Physics Department at Kent State University.

Abu Madi published three books of poetry in the United States, the last two considered his best: *al-Jadawil* (*The Brooks*, 1927), and *al-Khama'il* (*The Thickets*, 1940). Though she is often addressed in his work, Dora Diab Madey never read one of her husband's poems (knowing no Arabic).

The short poems here are translated for the first time in English, and his noted "Riddles" appears in a book full-length in English for the first time.

From Gratitude

What is poetry?
I have never seen two persons who do not quarrel about it.
Some say it is "inspiration revealed by God."
Others, "sputter from Satan."
Both err.
Nothing has urged man to poetry like "Man."
Man loves himself in others,
and loves "Man" in the universe.
For his sake I have built my palaces,
and paved the roads with sweet basil.
For his sake I have poured out my wines
and have tightened the strings of my lutes.
For his sake I have come back from the garden
with colors in my hands.
For his sake I have borrowed the jubilation
from the brook in the valley,
the laughter of pleasure from the streams,
—and, at sunset and sunrise—
the melting silver and gold from the sun.
We, the people of imagination,
are the happiest of God's creation,
even in times of deprivation.
How often we renounced the wealth of gold
and were satisfied with the wealth of aspirations,
vanishing in a procession of light,
shining in a flood of smoke.
When we thirst,
and water is out of reach,
the thought of creeks quenches our craving.
And when the stars disappear,
we are guided by dreams, by hope, by faith.
Mortals should not count our nights;
we are a people who live throughout time.

—Translated by George Dimitri Selim

HOLIDAY PRESENT

My angel!
What shall I give you as a present
for the holiday
when you have everything?
A bracelet of pure gold?
No! I hate fetters around your wrists.
Wines?
There is no wine on earth
like the wine which pours from your eyes.
Flowers?
The most beautiful flowers are those
I have smelled on your cheeks.
Carnelians, blazing like my heart?
But the precious carnelians are in your lips.
I have nothing dearer than my soul.
It lies pawned in your hands.

—Translated by George Dimitri Selim

THE SILENT TEAR

She heard the mourners wailing one night
in the neighborhood, awakening grief,
crying in the darkness over a young girl.
Wailing over youth is bitter . . .

After sorrow had stripped her of her smile, she said:
"He who said that life is a delusion is right.
Is this how we die,
how our dreams disappear in an instant,
and to dust we return?
And the worms of the earth rage in hearts
where hopes used to surge and stir?
More fortunate than us, then,

are those who were not born,
and better than men are boulders and rocks."

She stopped. I felt, after her talk,
the world confused and fragmented.
The summer was blowing its heat around us
and yet I felt as if I were suffering from cold.
She had driven doubt into my heart,
poisoning my night.
Where doubts are, there is no happiness . . .

I answered her:
"Let our bodies be for the worms of the earth!
Bodies are but shells.
Don't be afraid. Death won't harm us.
After death we will return.
Resurrection awaits us.
When mortals cease to be
and this visible world vanishes
we will still remain . . .
You will return as a fragrant thicket;
within it I will be an enchanted nightingale,
singing for you and hovering about,
making you smile . . .
Or you will return as a sparkling and melodious brook
whose laughing ripple and murmur I will be;
or as a breeze, forever circling the hills,
whose whisper and rustle I will be . . . "

She smiled. Satisfaction appeared on her face,
for she liked both the example and the image.
I cured her with delusion. She became happy.
Drugs often help the one in pain . . .

But when I went to sleep
my bed felt rough to me, though it was smooth . . .
By mounting sorrow
my heart was robbed of its dream,
my eyelid of its sleep.

Both were wronged by this death.
Doubts hovered around me
as if I were prey and they the hawks.
I resorted to hope but it would not obey me.
Imagination failed; it was defeated.

Oh night! I have lost my way.
Let there be light, if it exists!
Is this how we die,
how our dreams disappear in an instant,
and to dust we return?
More fortunate than us, then,
are those who were not born,
and better than men are stones and rocks.

—Translated by George Dimitri Selim

EAT AND DRINK!

Eat and drink, O you rich,
though the hungry fill the streets.
Dress in new silk,
though the poor wear rags.
Surround your palaces with men,
and surround your men with fortresses.
You will not see the victims of hunger;
and they will not see what you are doing.
If their existence inconveniences you,
and it troubles you that they cry,
order the soldiers to attack them.
That will teach them how death devastates.
They are aggressors,
criminals,
disturbers,
rebels.
Those clubs are for their heads,
those spears for their stomachs.
And those prisons, for whom did you build them

if you do not throw them in jail?
Order the sword to mow their heads:
such is the work of kings.
If soldiers do not guard you—
you the elite of the land—
whom are they going to guard?
If they do not kill the villains,
I wonder whom they are going to kill?
Do not grieve over their death
for they were born to perish.
And say: "Such was God's will.
What God decrees comes to pass."

*

And you poor!
Why do you complain?
Are you not ashamed?
Are you not embarrassed?
Leave the rich and their pleasures.
Like their pleasures, they are passing.
They will be in Hell forever.
In Paradise you will rejoice.
You will not thirst,
nor will you hunger.
They will not quench their thirst,
nor eat their fill.
For yours alone is the Kingdom of Heaven.
How is it you are not content?
Do not be sad because you are sleepless.
You shall sleep your fill.
You will recline with the prophets,
shaded by green branches.
A fragrant brilliance will surround you;
wine will run like rivers and sources.
Beautiful houris will serve you drink—
as they desire,
as you desire.

Such was God's promise to pious people;
and you are them, O tired ones.
Do you not believe what the Book says?
Woe to you!
You are unbelievers!

—Translated by George Dimitri Selim

THE BOMB OF ANNIHILATION

When the bomb pulverizes our earth
as the stone crushes the mustard seed,
and its impact razes the mountains
into rattling dust,
when annihilation creeps among the birds,
the walking animals, the crawling reptiles,
down to the last link of created life,
when it permeates all green things
eradicating them
so that no flowers are fragrant in the garden,
and no rooster crows on the dunghill
and time and its measure are lost
and the end resembles the beginning
and no living thing is spared on the surface of the earth
and Azrael no longer has any occupation:
this is disaster
the thought of which terrifies souls
before they experience it.
Yet one thing consoles us
when the bomb smashes our earth:
death will spare no human being
to blame others for the massacre!

—Translated by George Dimitri Selim

RIDDLES

I came,
Not knowing
My feet saw the way,
And I walked there,
And I shall continue
Whether I so desire or not.
How did I come?
How see the path?
  I know not.

Old or new,
Is this existence?
Am I free
Or fettered?
Do I lead myself
Or am I led?
I wish I knew.
  I do not.

And my path—
What is it?
Long or short?
Am I ascending or descending
And sinking deeper?
Is it I who travel
Along this path?
Or are we two stopped
And time that moves?
  I do not know.

Would that I knew!
While in the safe and unseen
Did I know, think you?
Think you
That before I was born a man

I was nothing
Or was I something?
Is there an answer
To this riddle?
Or must it be forever
unsolved?
I do not know;
And why I do not know
I know not.

In The Monastery

I was told
In the monastery are people
Who understood the mystery of life.
Yet there I found nothing
But stagnant minds
And corpse-like hearts
Where desire was worn out.
I am not blind.
Are others?
I don't know.

It has been said
That those best acquainted with
life's secrets
Are the hermitage dwellers.
I say, if this saying be true,
Then the secret is commonly known.
Strange, how veiled eyes
Can see the light
While the unveiled
Cannot.
I do not know.

I entered the monastery
To question the monks
Only to find them
As bewildered and amazed

As I am myself. Despair
Overcame them
And found them submissive.
Lo, on the door
Is written:
  I do not know.

Strange it is
That the recluse,
The all-knowing one,
Should abandon mankind
When among them
Is the beauty of God
For which he went
Searching in the desert;
What found he there,
Water or mirage?
  I do not know.

Recluse,
How often have you disputed the truth.
Had God intended
When He made you
That you should not love things beautiful,
He would have created you
Without heart or soul.
Then is it evil what you are doing?
He said:
  I do not know.

Fugitive,
It is disgrace to run away.
Surely no good will come
Of what you are doing,
Even to the wilderness.
You are guilty,
A criminal
With no reason for revenge.

Shall God approve
Or forgive?
  I do not know.

The Sea

I asked the sea,
Do I come from you?
Is it true
What some say
Of you and me?
Or is it a lie?
The waves laughed
And called:
  I do not know.

Sea,
How many centuries
Have passed over you?
Does the shore know
It is kneeling before you?
And the rivers, do they know
They are rushing back to you?
Whence did they come?
What was it the angry waves said?
  I do not know.

Sea,
You send the clouds
Which water land and trees.
We ate you
And said
We ate fruit.
We drank of you
And said
We drank the rain.
Is this true or false?
  I don't know.

Sea,
I asked the clouds
If they remembered your sands,
The leafy trees,
Your kindly rains,
And the pearls
Their birthplace.
Together I heard them say:
  I don't know.

The waves dance.
Yet in your depths
A ceaseless war is waged.
There you made fish
And ravenous whale.
To your bosom
You have gathered
Life and death;
Are you cradle or tomb?
  I do not know.

How many a lad and maid,
Like Leyla
And ibn-ul-Mullawah,
Spent hours on your shore,
Listening and confessing
In ecstatic strains
Their love.
Is the sound of the waves
A lost secret?
  I don't know.

How many kings at night
Built pleasure domes
Beside you!
Then morning came
And found nothing but mist.
Will they return, these kings?
Are they deep in the sand?

The sand said:
  I don't know.

In you, sea,
Shellfish and sand.
Shadow nor mind have you.
And I have both.
Why should I die?
And you live?
  I do not know.

Oh, book of time,
Has time past or future?
I am in time
As a small boat
On a boundless sea.
Have I no goal?
Has time?
Oh, for knowledge!
But how?
  I do not know.

Sea,
In my breast
Are many secrets
A veil fell over.
And I am the veil.
The nearer I come,
The farther away I am.
When I seem
About to understand,
  I do not.

I am a sea, too,
Whose shores are yours,
The unknown tomorrow
And yesterday.
And you and I
Are but a drop

In the fathomless deep.
Don't ask
What is tomorrow,
What is yesterday.
I know not.

—Translated by Andrew Ghareeb

BE A BALM

Be a balm when time turns into a speckled snake,
sweetness when others turn to bitterness.
Life has given you all its treasures;
do not then be miserly with its gifts.
Do good, though you may not be recompensed
by a word of thanks.
What reward does rain expect when it falls?
Who rewards the scent-giving flower?
Who repays the singing nightingale?
My friend! Learn love from them,
a precious lesson I have found.
Strive for the happiness of others
if you wish to be happy in life.
Awaken your feelings with love if they slumber.
Were it not for feelings people would be robots.
Love, and the hut becomes a bright world;
hate, and the world turns into a dungeon.
Without wine, the cup is only glass;
Without love, man is but bones.
If you love the desert,
its sand becomes flowers,
its deceptive mirage becomes water.
When beauty appears to the intelligent man
he loves it.
The sight of beauty brings suspicion
in the ignorant man
and he stones it.
Do not ask for love from the ignorant;

man does not love until he understands.
And be kind to the children of stupidity
as though they were ill—
ignorance is akin to blindness.
Turn your attention from the thorns
to the garden flowers,
and forget the scorpions when you see the stars.

—Translated by George Dimitri Selim

ETEL ADNAN

(1925–)

Etel Adnan

Born in 1925 in Beirut, Lebanon, Etal Adnan explains, "Looking west at the sunsets it was natural that I would have a life of explorations, journeys, and exiles."

A prolific writer and critic of life in contemporary Arab society, Adnan is also an artist whose childhood vacations spent in the gardens around Damascus, and in later times "falling in love" in the rose gardens of the Palazzo Pitti in Florence, brought her to comment, "Chasing sceneries or maybe the sun I also became a painter." Her artwork has been exhibited in Washington, D.C.

Adnan has published five collections of poetry in English and two in French, the most recent being *L'Apocalypse Arabe* (1980), *Pablo Neruda Is a Banana Tree* (1982) and *The Indian Never Had a Horse* (1985). Among her poetry and fiction which have appeared in periodicals in Lebanon, France, and the United States is the William Gass-inspired story based on the Lebanese Civil War "In the Heart of the Heart of Another Country," published in *Mundis Artium* (1977). She is also the author of a novel, *Sitt Marie Rose* (1977), and a book of poetic contemplations, *Journey to Mount Tamalpais* (1986). Adnan has appeared in numerous anthologies, including *For Neruda, For Chile* (1975), *Women of the Fertile Crescent* (1978), and *And Not Surrender* (1982).

Adnan taught philosophy at the Dominican College of San Raphael in California from 1959 to 1972 and now divides her time between Sausalito, across the Golden Gate Bridge, and Paris, France.

"The All-Pervasive Thing"

I began writing poetry because nothing else in my adolescence interested me. It was in Beirut and for awhile the sea permeated absolutely everything. I was being in love with the sea, and the sun was everywhere, and I felt that the sun had more divine presence than all the nonsense taught in school about religion or morality. I saw that the sea and the sun were first woman and first man, first being and first present to me, and that was my first poem. Then every time something appeared to be the most important thing, the all-pervasive thing, I wrote about it and such things are called poems.

To be an Arab is already being a bit an American. And being an American is already being almost an Arab, even without knowing it. Americans are a nomadic people. Arabs are a nomadic and restless people. Both are restless and reckless. Because Americans are nomadic they could but go to the moon. And Arabs were astronomers and mathematicians and opened the new age—the age that made it possible later to go to the moon and to go to the stars.

But poetry does not have a place in American society because American society is alienated from itself. Americans are storytellers and they are often poets: visual poets, language poets, visionaries, delinquents, street poets, mad poets. But poetry has no place in American society because this society which is American is living under thick clouds of advertisings, and the metaphysical insecurity which makes great poetry is buried under a thick cloud of government-induced and market-induced and doctor-induced insecurity.

Still you can hear American poets in your sleep. And knocking at your door.

THE BEIRUT-HELL EXPRESS

. . . but there are different treatises
always taken again as a heritage
in which, like tired continents, great
figures closed into their insanity have sunk . . .

—Malek Alloula, *"Villes," Algiers '68*

The human race is going to the cemetery
in great upheavals

two horses reciting MAO

my uneasiness
to be heroic

bread and roses
flowers and flames

Gamal Abdel Nasser's death is
lived in the universe of
JAZZ Mingus's bass
shocks with no return
what to do with wonder if not
some pain in the head one California
night the road and black
trees against which are rubbing
their faces two men in waiting? . . .

taxi drivers urinate standing
on the Damascus-Beirut-Damascus
road
inglorious itinerary
I inhabit the tiniest country
in an expanding universe

I love the women who are veiled
like my aunt used to be
and those who go naked
at the American crossroads where
drugs are growing: they are
crabs lying on the back of
starfish in the sea

I love the men who cover their
head and show but one eye
not the blind one but the one
which looks inside.
From two thousand years of History I
keep but JAZZ
because it is Black. I banished
colors and dried up the sea
here you only eat sand . . .
we all are torturers
one shadowless morning
one morning!
Don't you know that I live
in San Rafael with San Quentin for neighbor
a nightmare on which the sun
sets in tears
the Bay at its feet and
the moon . . . it's always she
rising above the hair
of a woman four times suicidal
and an island a single one
Angel Island uninhabited
and in the Prison
George Jackson and Sirhan Sirhan
a cold nail
enters the skin
20,000 dead in Amman
20,000 shining nails around the head
of the King
20,000 ghosts heavy weights stinking
the air crime the autumn of the criminal.

The flag of prophecy floats on
the ships
Fire! let the hurricane enter
the holes and like a boiling river
carry away the angels stricken with fear
on the summits of the Sannine!
move on people full of slime
let your lemonades go to the sea
let your casino crumble
let your race horses carry their owners
to those undergrounds where Babylon
used to cook its poisons

liberation like a spring still
under the ground is growing what
seems to be hands open at the level
of the soil there is no grass on this earth.

My father was Ouranos
and my mother Queen Zenobia
I am the initial Fish
rejected on the beach
but determined to live.

Do you know imbeciles that Rimbaud
was among us a century ago
from Beirut to Aden-Arabia
and that Fouad Gabriel Naffah the poet
I repeat Fouad Gabriel Naffah
is among us
crucified by your thickness
burned with nitrogen
yes people of Beirut go on
snoring let nitrate burn
these pine-tree forests where
you throw your garbage your paper towels
the country is the dumpsite
for the foreign merchandise
that everyone refuses

Tammouz's country is an
open sore
his degenerate descendants
have their shoes shined
by the hands of a herd of beggars
                    you borrowed your masks
                    from the pigs and the cows
there have been three earthquakes
in the Third century
destroying three times Beirut
and a fourth one is coming!

the world is being born
the people are coming
the people are coming
        the eagle has carried the message
                to the tribe
        the camel has carried the message
                to the tribe
        the shark has carried the message
                to the tribe

from everywhere in the world they are
        coming.
The Revolution is coming . . .

In New York I say the hell with America
In Moscow I say the hell with Stalin
In Rabat I say the hell with Hassan II

        hello the beggar
        hello to the fedai
        hello to Mohammad the visionary
        hello to the prisoner

In the evening when darkness moves
        as slow as mud
I watch the prostitutes
        it is forbidden that women
        think

I watch our servants
it is forbidden that women go
to sleep
I watch our brides
going to bed alone
it is forbidden that women
lie as gazelles
on the infinite fields of the Arabian plains

On the fields
on the Arabian plains
on the face of the desert
on the streets of our
bitch-in-heat cities
there are only
the maimed
and governments with no end
crime barks higher than
hyenas
BABYLON BABYLON
I announce your resurrections
and your death.
We shall go from the Resistance
to the psychic conquest

and then to prophecy

and from the prophecy to the divine
the divine is the people-who-suffer

Comrade Dostoevsky
is in Beirut he stays
at the Orient-Prince Hotel, he
eats at the Horseshoe cafe
he swims—you're not kidding—
at the St. George he yawns
—imagine that!—at the A.U.B.
and for his redemption he counts
the typographical errors of the
daily an-Nahar

Comrade Dostoevsky
enjoys but the Koran
understands but compassion

Comrade Dostoevsky
is arrested by the Security Service
and he laughs laughs and his laughter
is broadcast on the radios of
the whole world
I caught it on channel 14
in California

O how I would like to break the sky
and provoke the lightning
bring down the deluge on this
town!
Calmly we have prostituted
even the plants Vulture-faced
sorrow is crying
while the boat refuses to leave

In the middle of History
In the heart of the hexagon
at the leverage point of the
building
at the meeting spot
of honor

lives and dies
Gamal Abdel Nasser

and his grave witnesses its
first miracle

I am going to talk to you
about the moslem saints: and the naked
girls lying by our dead . . .

It is in Jabal Amman
that you should look for resurrection

it is in the Wahdat Camp
that you should look for spring
it is on the bones of Abou Sliman
that you should write koranic
        verses

City more unreal than the wind
although pregnant with the sins of
        the world
it is in your belly that foreigners
exercise the alchemy of treason

                I love the October breeze
                the red skies which foretell
                the coming wars
                above the sea
                acetylene lamps light
                the fishermen and the
                boats . . .

Hamra Street: our nerves shrink at this name
        blood becomes white the pedestrian
        becomes a ghost the Lebanese pound
        exudes a stench

        and I fall on my knees
        in front of the children we sell
        for the pleasure of some night
        for the afternoon pleasure or
        the four in the morning one sadism
        costs so little in Beirut

City! how many crimes in your bars how
much alcohol in the fountains of the old houses
what a monetary orgy in the call of the
muezzin!

city more famous than hell
passenger of all passages
eldest daughter of all trade

object of our nocturnal love
you have intoxicated us with
your irremediable purity.

The tempest has come
the trumpet has sounded JAZZ is
manifested delirium has advanced the hour
the hour the hour has stopped we
are naked destiny is there in front
Gilgamesh has eaten his secret plant

people of Beirut covered with numbers
swimming in butter numbed
with evil thoughts

remember September the 18th!

a motorized angel has crossed the sky

break your mirrors
look toward Mount Sannine
look at the sun which is emerging
new

bring our your swords
cut open the Arabian gut
from side to side
let freedom explode!

I have spontaneous funerary orations
for the metals: no sulfur
or manganese but potassium
chloride in the water for the donkeys
and mortuary chalk on the
houses

traitors the painters: they plunge
in buckets of acid

traitors the poets: they speak of roses
                    when the city is an
                    asphalt garden
traitors the officials: they have as umbilical
                    cords the telephone lines
                    that link them to Washington
                    Vladivostok
traitors the priests: there is a business shuttle
                    in the schools and consciences
                    covered with vermin
let liberation liberate!

City!

            you are at the foot of the
                    pink mountain and each one of us
                    is a legend

One out of two bums is covered with lice
what a velvet on his tender skin a live
hair young men coming out of the Empire
Cinema with swollen lips masturbation in
the dark atavistic hunger installed in
the belly the smell of the film becoming
woman the big desert of love is going
to cover them in the grave already made
they only know how to love their mother . . .

I know streets where the police
rape anything going on two feet

                    the sons of the rich
                    go by them in speedy cars
                    glassy eyed cold
                              stone
I would like to announce the fabulous
acceleration of the planets and the
dynamics of catastrophe: sons of Canaanites
you are dying for the very last time

Take a train, my friend, the train
for Amman
        "it is the only place on earth
        which proposes to us an occult
        life and proposes it at the surface
        of life"

        it is Antonin Artaud who is saying it

        Our fate is the one
        of the Red Indian: the oiliferous
        hordes are going to destroy the very
        banks they built as numerous as chimneys

        we have mornings with no memories

I predict a tidal wave
        dried up well
        anthill a southern wart
        is gnawing
at the land formerly said of the Ancestor

We have perspired at noon an
icy sweat   we have seen thieves
met on the sidewalk an astronaut wearing
a wig   our housewives have skins which
are burned   nitroglycerine bags put in the
frontal lobe of their lovers explode under
the fatuous laughter of the enemy

        Beirut is a witch-city
        which acts on the world
        as an ill omen

What to do with innocence if not
a parade like a face tumor
one night with a strong light
in California the road and the beach

the black trees against which
Ahmad-the-Violence and Khalil-Debauchery
rub their phallus because they are
scared scared scared of the Express
train which is carrying away their
double at fast speed

a speed
of death
in the dry
ravines
of the city
which is burned
with American phosphorus

It has been a million years
since the Hashemites left
Mecca in the belly of the first
dinosaur to finish up in this
massacre!

It has been a million years
since Amman-Ugliness
has been condemned on the throne
of the Apocalypse of the Oil.

I took a long walk on Beirut's Corniche
with Al-Ghazali as a companion

I took olive oil in the Greek
churches and anointed him
Prince of the City

Comrade al-Ghazali
stays at the Metropol
eats at Barmaki's chats with
his Lebanese friends of the
theatre at Wimpy's and receives

his mail care of Interpol
His own letters are sent by
a traveling whale

they play the flute in the
popular quarters of the city
in order to quiet down the anger
of the citizens . . .

The god Shamash has come back
in Irbid
in Zarka
In Ur and in
Basrah

the dead are coming back in order to fight again
because the living are cowards!

people of Beirut
in bikinis in slips
covered with feathers if
need be
take the first Express

(take your vertebrae and squeeze out
colonialism like pus)

so that there be
air

so that there be
water

so that there be
earth

so that there be
fire

take the Beirut——Hell Express
take the Express
it is more than too late
the train is whistling stamping spitting
the Beirut——Hell Express.

1970

From JOURNEY TO MOUNT TAMALPAIS

Sometimes, they open a new highway, and let it roll, open wide the earth, shake trees from their roots. The Old Woman suffers once more. Birds leave the edges of the forest, abandon the highway. They go up to mountain tops and from the highest peaks they take in the widest landscapes, they even foresee the space age.

*

Like a chorus, the warm breeze had come all the way from Athens and Baghdad, to the Bay, by the Pacific Route, its longest journey. It is the energy of these winds that I used, when I came to these shores, obsessed, followed by my home-made furies, errynies, and such potent creatures. And I fell in love with the immense blue eyes of the Pacific: I saw its red algae, its blood-colored cliffs, its pulsating breath. The ocean led me to the mountain.

*

The ocean is launching its brilliant waves against the asphalt-black walls of the mountain and in the night of this ocean I am finding the freshness of dispersed springs. Harbors catch fire at the edge of the sea. Everything, at last, is upside down. The skies are confused with blackness and water is green like eyes which are cruel and opened on smoke.

*

The Indian called the Mountain Tamal-Pa, "The One close to the Sea." The Spaniard called it Mal-Pais, "Bad Country"! The difference between the native and the conqueror is readable in these two different perceptions of the same reality. Let us be the Indian and let be! What is close to the sea shall remain close to the sea.

*

It had snowed. Tamalpais was white as it rarely is. White is the color of terror in this century: the great white mushroom, the white and radiating clouds, the White on White painting by Malevich, and that whiteness, most fearful, in the eyes of men.

Television is white, pale as God: an infinite amount of channels masterminding everything, projecting the antlike destinies of us all. The mountain is its opposite: aloof, waiting for us all to go to it, innocent.

*

Through the long night of the species we go on, somehow blindly, and we give a name to our need for a breakthrough: we call it the Angel, or call it Art, or call it the Mountain.

*

I will always remember the day Ranger 8 hit the moon. It was a Saturday in February. It sent back the first close-ups of the craters and of a face which was pocked, rubbery, like burning milk breaking up in bubbles, stretching its skin. We felt like we were sitting within that strange lunar smile making fun of earthbound creatures.

On the same television program appeared Red China's first nuclear explosion and I saw not only a mushroom-like form, but a human brain. It was like the birth of the human brain under our very eyes.

*

I am sitting as usual in front of Mount Tamalpais. I can't get over its deep greens.

It is clear. It is empty. My spirit is anguished by color. Color is the sign of the existence of life. I feel like believing, being in a state of pure belief, of affirmation. I exist because I see colors. Sometimes, at other moments, it is as if I didn't exist, when colors seem foreign, unreachable, impregnable fortresses. But there is no possession of color, only the acceptance of its reality. And if there is no possibility of color, there is no possession at all. Of whatever it is.

D. H. MELHEM

(1926–)

D. H. Melhem

D. H. (Diana Helen) Melhem was born in Brooklyn to Greco- and Syro-Lebanese immigrants. She raised her two children on Manhattan's West Side, where she has resided for many years. Her childhood home was filled with music and poetry; her mother's own poem written on Ellis Island in 1922 ends the book-length work *Rest in Love* (1975, 1978) excerpted here. As Melhem describes the early atmosphere, "My father recited incantatory Arabic poetry and sang hymns in Arabic and English. My mother read aloud from Whittier and from Longfellow's *Hiawatha*. I remember my parents cranking an august Victrola out of which Caruso and John McCormack would magically issue."

Two of Melhem's poetry books deal with her "longtime Muse, the multiethnic West Side." They are *Notes on 94th Street* (1972, 1979) and *Children of the House Afire* (1976). Recipient of a National Endowment for the Humanities fellowship, her Ph.D. dissertation at the City University of New York began her ten-year study, *Gwendolyn Brooks: Poetry and the Heroic Voice* (University Press of Kentucky, 1987). Among many articles published, one is the award-winning account of her former husband's recovery from a stroke (*New York Times Magazine*, March 11, 1979).

Melhem has been a member of the faculty at Long Island University and the New School for Social Research; she retains the title of adjunct professor at the Union for Experimenting Colleges and Universities. Currently she is at work on a critical study of six contemporary black poets, two new poetry collections, and a musical drama about the West Side.

Some Notes on Origins

In my immigrant parents' world, Syrian, Serbian, and Siberian were equal curiosities, easily confused.

In Brooklyn, I grew up a Protestant in an Irish and Italian Catholic neighborhood, then a Christian in a Jewish neighborhood. Baptized Greek Orthodox and confirmed as a Lutheran (the Protestant church nearest our house), imbued with pride in my cultural heritage, I also considered myself in turn an honorary Catholic, Jew, Briton, Native American, and, later, black, according to the backgrounds of my friends and my own deep interests. Although I loved my friends—always of other cultures (no Middle Easterners around)—at times I was made acutely aware of our differences. I think of Richard Wright, who appreciated the value of his enforced introspection, but sometimes envied the relatively uncomplicated state of white children's awareness.

I was raised in a United Nations atmosphere. My mother and her sisters would shift—for secrecy or linguistic exercise—from English to Arabic to French to Greek. My grandmother spoke these languages plus German (an orphan, she had been educated by Prussian nuns) and enjoyed radio newscasts. My aunts and one of my uncles married (respectively) a German, a Pole, a Belgian Frenchman, an Englishman, an Irishwoman, and then a German-Irish American. I believed, and still do, with Socrates and Tom Paine, that one is ultimately a citizen of the world. Yet America lives for me and for my family, past and present, in Lincoln's vision: "the last, best hope of earth."

My maternal grandmother was born in Beirut. I began to see myself in the context of an anguished reality that overwhelmed benign past echoes. The Palestinians seemed terribly wronged; peaceable Lebanon had again become the battleground for conflicting foreign interests. The 1982 massacres at Sabra and Shatila that shook the world filled me with grief and rage. My kaffiyeh, given me by a Palestinian on the September Washington march, became my emblem.

Since ethnic aspects mirror economic and political forces, to be ethnic in a political void is an unaffordable luxury. If, however, poets cannot shape their concerns into good poetry, they may acknowledge their relation to society in other ways. And if they can *write effectively, let them wield their poems like cedar branches, bury discrimination and injustice in grape leaves and olive boughs. Let the* oud *and* durbakkah *prophesy over the tomb their triumph of art and life.*

LAMENTATION AFTER JEREMIAH TO EXORCISE HIGH RENTAL / HIGH RISE BUILDING SCHEDULED FOR CONSTRUCTION WITH PUBLIC FUNDS

solitary city
you weep in the night
over treacherous friends
become enemies
your people sigh
they seek bread

I have lived in
your affliction
it has soured my flesh
battered my bones
it has hedged me about and made my chain heavy
it lies in wait as insatiable lions
in public places

here on this street where
steel grows in a hard ground
fitted with floors of implacable profit
cool as coins
in high pride standing upon
unimportant bodies

rich building
woe unto you if you rise here
this critical space will cave you
into the cave of its cries

GRANDFATHER: FRAILTY IS NOT THE STORY

for Dana and Gregory

Remember your grandfather tall and straight
Remember him swimming in deep water
Remember his stories of exile and travel
  and immigrant dreams
Remember his ship models designed from memory
Remember him netting shiners with you in Gardiner's Bay
  or digging for clams
  or cleaning a fish
  or driving us fast
  to catch the sunset at Maidstone.

I remember him climbing the stairs
  after all the stairs he had climbed
  with his satchel of fabrics
I remember him on stepladders in the Depression
  or holding my hand on the way to school
  me proud of him in his overalls
I remember watching for him at six o'clock
  he would lift me at the door
and then we would sit over roast lamb shanks or chicken
and my mother would relate the family news.
Afterwards he would rise to "stretch his legs,"
  read the paper, and doze.

And I remember discussions, the arguments over politics
  how he taught me to reason, to wield logic
  as he had done when captain of the debating team
  in Tripoli Boys' School, Lebanon
  and the photos of him there, where he was becoming
  the tallest and handsomest man in the town.

I remember the pipes arrayed like sentinels on a cabinet
the talk of building or buying a boat

explanations of algebra, which I learned to enjoy
and the excursions—
  walking over Brooklyn Bridge into Chinatown
  walking down Ocean Parkway to Sheepshead Bay
or later in a Ford, the three of us, singing
  of the San Fernando Valley
  where we would settle down
  and never more roam.

Remember your grandfather
in his vigor
and that a loving life
takes imagination.

TO AN ETHIOPIAN CHILD

When you sang the clear water of your mother's womb
she blessed your body with the cry of her thighs.
Strong as a river, she floated you on her stomach,
she floated you on her back. With her hands
she cleft the air clean for your breath.
You were born to the sun, to the opal sky,
to the fig and pomegranate and apricot,
korareema, sansevieria,
to the cotton for your shehma,
to the red blossoms of the Kosso tree,
to the mimosa and myrrh that fragrance you.

Why does the sun yield no day to rain,
beat back grain to the ground?
Your water song gurgles the air.
You drink your tears.
Your mother bleeds milk into your mouth.
She claws the earth
to find you a porridge of mud.

Can you eat your heritage down to the stones?
Can you eat those stones down to bedrock?

Can you chew the baga, the dry season?
Wait for keuramt to come. Wait for monsoon
to anoint the tableland.

Your face that lifts from newspapers
looks out at me from TV.
Who is this plucked bird, fly-specked?
Who is this skull on a stick?

Your mother leans from the screen.
She wrenches you from her empty breast
and sets you on my table. Your hand
rests on mine that presses the gravy spoon
into mashed potatoes, leaving a brown pool.
You wait, then slip back
into TV, where
your mother holds you again.
She brushes flies from your open eyes.

The picture flickers with heat,
flickers with dust
into a dry assembly of skulls,
increasing,
flickering.

From REST IN LOVE

It was warm in Grandma's kitchen. Throughout this, her second apartment in the New World, the fiery steam heat rises with dawn and dinner from the coal-stoked furnace in the basement, but the kitchen is warmed all day by the cooking and washing. My mother, my grandmother, sit at the white enamel kitchen table, kneading dough, shelling peas, measuring pine nuts into the chopped lamb and onions, soaking the crushed wheat for kibbeh, filling dozens of meat pies, stuffing chicken and squash and green peppers and egg-plant, rolling stuffed grape leaves and stuffed cabbage like cigars, making dumplings for yoghurt soup among cans of sesame oil and boiled butter, peeling scores of potatoes for baked lamb necks and shanks and roast chicken, boiling rice, browning rice and onions, adding rice and tomatoes to large pots of marrow-bone vegetable soup, sitting and chatting over familiar tasks that are done must be done will be done every day without respite, my mother, my grandmother at the kitchen table with me between them on a stool in the corner where I watch and listen, tasting dough and stuffing, rewards for being content to observe and accept, with my silence, their love.

Waiting for them to acknowledge me, I absorb the strange names of relatives and friends I shall never meet, Beit this and Beit that, houses remote as the house of Atreus, incidents and characters recalled and savored as I anticipate the mention of meaningful names dropping from the flow of Arabic between them: aunts and uncles who live in the house, my mother's sisters and brothers.

And I bear witness to a daily translation of two women's lives into pots and pans, the circumscription of kitchen walls, with heat rising amid the smells and rhythm of effort, into patterns and patience, interchangeable days carried by movements worn to such precision that hand and object extend each other. How many times does the body yearn beyond clothesline and tar roof? Dough sticks to fingers; clock hands restrain.

*

long through your hand
broom handle moves
upon sandtrails
of summer feet

sunlit shoulders
bent over dustpan
straighten at me
you smile

sufficient, here
to be

*

Death is the flower whose shadow petals open slowly upon their secret.

Her face, in that last moment, pale, reduced to a dove's serenity, flickered a frown, a puzzlement (surely death always surprises) as if, were she able to speak she would have uttered a final, "No!"

I put my face against her cheek. I wept, and held her. She was warm, but never again would she lift her arms to me.

The secret in that flower of death is longing. I waited. I took her blue coat in my arms.

*

I found
the little book of poems, *Rest*,
in which you had written at seventeen
traveling here on the *Homeric*,
lines about life
in small letters:

> *Lives begin*
> *at different times*
> *and in places separated*
> *from one another*
> *by magnanimous distances*
> *and yet they cross each other*
> *at some point running on together*
> *then breaking off again,*
> *until arriving*
> *at that inevitable point—Death.*
> *It is at those crossings that we find*
> *momentary happiness which may continue*
> *or we may find the beginning*
> *of sorrow and unrest . . .*

Woolworth snapshots
throughout:

in the little book of poems
my pictures

*

the red silk rose I gave you
relinquished into the bud vase with my own
is joined by a third rose, brightly
gregory made it of aluminum foil

stems
touch

*

rainstopped
inchworm suspended from whiteoak

the trees are a permanent green

thrasher comes
and phoebe nesting

how still it remains
anguish so deep it is almost serene

*

your pine nuts/her chestnuts
one dressing
communion with dead mothers
continues the circling
turkey platters

yams   creamed onions   dana's cranberry sauce
greg's mincemeat   my pie crust

filled with the empty spaces
at table
every remembrance goes round
fruit at the center

*

you died of goodness   that disease
affecting primarily   females
brought upright to respect
their elders   patted flat

*

in your multitudinous self
there was no self
but the poet composed
for others

*

I am the life my mother wanted
I feel her in my womb
that wise child

hand on her knee
remembers
textures
step remembers
her direction

face in my hands
longs for her lap

even her apron
loved me

*

Tonight I ate from my childhood
lamb and chick peas and yoghurt
gulping it hot
as I sat alone in the kitchen
gorging on my own dead flesh,
it seemed.

Nobody came back. Not one word
of Arabic. Only my spoon
tapping my plate.
And the hot food poured into me
a bonfire of recollections
and my eyes burned with all
the deadly heat of it
as I foolishly expected
to enjoy my reminiscence
privately, whole.

I finished my coffee,
and went to sleep
in an overheated room
the dog under my bed
and awoke, the darkness having
pulled down memory
to a quest for slippers
and the bathroom.

*

Ellis Island
September 25, 1922

Ellis Island to you I cry
Within my deep griefs and sorrow
Even through clouds high in the sky
Shall thy swelling, rough heart still grow
Hard, like a flint stone?

Your bosom is full of small pinks,
Yet you are active in your deed:
Shall I cry through the chain that links
The souls of every age in need,
Shall thy heart be stone?

Under the sunshine, everywhere,
Even from the bloody fields of life
Lives cry to you, while you bear
The crown of rest out of strife,
Shall thy heart be stone?

Perfect care, fully protection,
While [. . .] from your bosom,
Look at the children in devotion
Cry sincerely, like a blossom
Shall thy heart be stone?

Oh! Like a rivulet floweth
Your perfect peace, while the sun shines,
And the dreary life endureth
Within the bulging heart that repines
Shall thy heart be stone?

Be patient, my soul and don't fail,
For the suffering brings fully rest
Through the prison-bars and dark jail.
Nay, sweet love may cry from its nest
Shall thy heart be stone?

—Georgette Deyratani Melhem

SAMUEL HAZO

(1928–)

Samuel Hazo

Founder of the renowned International Poetry Forum in Pittsburgh and one of the preeminent poets in America today, Samuel Hazo was born in 1928 in Pittsburgh to immigrant parents of Assyrian and Lebanese origin. Once nominated for the National Book Award, Hazo published a volume of his selected poems, *Thank a Bored Angel* (New Directions, 1983). His most recent novel is *Stills* (Athenlum, 1989).

Hazo trod many paths before poetry became his chief work. He was a debate champion at Notre Dame, a Captain in the U.S. Marine Corps, and a football, baseball and basketball coach, and then in 1965 professor of English at Duquesne University, where he still teaches.

His twelve books of poetry include *Blood Rights* (University of Pittsburgh Press, 1968), *Once for the Last Bandit* (University of Pittsburgh Press, 1972) and *To Paris* (New Directions, 1981). Hazo has published two other novels (*The Very Fall of the Sun*, Popular Library, 1977, and *The Wanton Summer Air*, North Point Press, 1982) and a collection of short fiction (*Inscripts*, University of Ohio Press, 1975). A book-length study of Hart Crane, *Smithereened Apart* (1977), is just one of many of Hazo's critical works that have also appeared in articles in the *New York Times*, *Hudson Review*, *Commonweal*, and *Mundus Artium*, among others. Hazo has collaborated in the translation of Adonis, the acclaimed Syrian poet, and the philosophic writings of Denis de Rougement.

Named Pittsburgh's Man of the Year in the Arts for 1984, Hazo has brought Nobel Laureates in Literature to the International Poetry Forum as well as actors, singers, dignitaries and others such as his close friend, the late Princess Grace of Monaco. Hazo himself has been on literary speaking tours in the Middle East and West Indies for the U.S. State Department.

Hazo resides with his wife, Mary Anne, and son, Samuel, Junior, in Pittsburgh.

"If He's Plucked"

I began writing poetry in college for reasons that remain mysterious to me, and I continue to write it because it is the only way I know to try to say what can't be said, which is for me the only thing worth saying. Being an American of Arabic origin has nothing to do with it and shouldn't and can't have. One writes out of what one is, and that is best done without self-consciousness. Let critics deal with the consequences. As for the place that poetry has in American life, suffice it to say that that place—based upon the people who read poetry—is marginal. Based upon the idea of America rather than upon sales and statistics, poetry is central. What is America but a poem—a dream of Jefferson's that is still evolving? How can poetry ever be divorced from that?

The simple fact is that understanding comes through language. Not through playing with language, not through pictures. You get recognition with pictures, not understanding. You can listen to a news broadcaster and he will give you news in the order of decreasing calamity, beginning with the most perfect. After two or three pieces he will stop and say, "More after this." And there will be a pause for a commercial and then he will come on with some more catastrophes. Poetry doesn't say that. Poetry says "Less after this" or "Nothing after this." After this, you wonder. You don't wait for more grist for your mill. You just want to say, hey, wait a minute. This particular thing changed me.

What the poet does is create a place for wonder or for doubt or silence or for nothing. You're not on the treadmill, engorging more and more information. Information is a neutral thing. Knowledge is a neutral thing, finally, unless you reach a point where it comes to wisdom. Then it's like vanity, we've been told. You can know everything, and if you don't have charity, you're nothing. And the poet, his vision is the kind of thing that, if he's right, if he's plucked, if he's inspired, if everything is working correctly, then even if only one person reads that poem and is different, he has succeeded.

THE TOYS

Wing to wing, they bake
in weather that can sizzle bacon
on their stars.
Fighters, bombers,
trainers—Arizona stores them all
unrusting in a prophecy of yesterday.
West by half the Pacific, the holy
salvage of another *Arizona*
consecrates Pearl Harbor like a church . . .
If wreckages were pages, nothing
could book them.
Cain's garbage
mines the Baltic, fouls
forty years of bracken near
Cassino, spoils Guam's lagoon.
What were these havocs to their crews
but new toys for an old game?
As facts left over from a fact,
they speak for history ahead
of all that history remembers
to predict about the tactics of our kind.
Cain's rock and rocket
leave us nothing new to find.
In North America the oldest skull's
a woman's, brained from behind.

SOME WORDS FOR PRESIDENT WILSON

Declaring war on Germany but not
its citizens, he took no enemy
for granted but Americans.
They

crippled him.
After his stroke,
he somehow kept his grin.
That,
his pince-nez and his Presbyterian
chin survived the lost
election and the sag of normalcy.
Blanketed and read to by a wife
rare men deserve, he thought
of Princeton, Trenton and the years
before Versailles . . .
He never guessed
that he would be the final
president to write his speeches
out by hand.
Or that
the future he foresaw but never
saw would happen differently
the same and change its wars
by number, not by name.

FOR FAWZI IN JERUSALEM

Leaving a world too old to name
and too undying to forsake,
I flew the cold, expensive sea
toward Columbus' mistake
where life could never be the same

for me. In Jerash on the sand
I saw the colonnades of Rome
bleach in the sun like skeletons.
Behind a convalescent home,
armed soldiers guarded no man's land

between Jordanians and Jews.
Opposing sentries frowned and spat.
Fawzi, you mocked in Arabic

this justice from Jehoshaphat
before you shined my Pittsburgh shoes

for nothing. Why you never kept
the coins I offered you is still
your secret and your victory.
Saying you saw marauders kill
your father while Beershebans wept

for mercy in their holy war,
you told me how you stole to stay
alive. You must have thought I thought
your history would make me pay
a couple of piastres more

than any shine was worth—and I
was ready to—when you said, "No,
I never take. I never want
America to think I throw
myself on you. I never lie."

I watched your young but old man's stare
demand the sword to flash again
in blood and flame from Jericho
and leave the bones of these new men
of Judah bleaching in the air

like Roman stones upon the plain
of Jerash. Then you faced away.
Jerusalem, Jerusalem,
I asked myself if I could hope
for peace and not recall the pain

you spoke. But what could hoping do?
Today I live your loss in no
man's land but mine, and every time
I talk of fates not just but so,
Fawzi, my friend, I think of you.

PITTSBURGH IN PASSING

Between old battles and the ones I should
be seeing, I have lost my circus eyes.
Birthdays are deathdays. I feel the glaciering
of centuries beneath the pulse of clocks
and through the blown-out candles of my blood.

I stand unarmed where Braddock's armies stood.
Instead of Hurons I see acres piped
and sewered for our waste and mined with bones
of Quakers, Indians and immigrants.
Three decades in the woods of William Penn

have left me kin to all the buried men
who claimed this wilderness and named this town.
Where Washington marched in buckskin, I can drive
through battlefields of signs and ironworks,
inhale unrevolutionary air

and damn the siren waking me to war-
alerts each Monday of the year. Senates
have bolstered us with bunkercaves and rockets.
A palisade of missiles rings the town
while banking and burlesque thrive back to back

in the same building. Threats of surprise attack
would bench a naked tease and the most correct
of tellers flank to flank in a joint shelter.
No one objects. Shielded around the clock
by minutemen in radar shacks, we tomb

the Hiroshima world beside old Rome
and older Troy while mayors fatten us
with talk. No one admits we walk on skulls,
and no one prays Isaiah back to speak
the truth without refining it to please!

The siren spins. The aborigines
and whites who battled here are six wars old.
Chained to a different blunderbluss, we sleep
in cemeteries screened by warhead forts
and dream our moats are still the seven seas.

THE WORLD THAT LIGHTNING MAKES

Under an upside-down
  and sooty ocean, I steer
  through summer thunder
  and the straight prose of rain.
A dashboard voice from Washington
  talks war in Lebanon . . .
                                        Bursting
  like rocketry, a scar of fire
  slashes down the sky.
                                        It noons
  the night and shocks me
  to a crawl.
                        My car's a shelter
  under siege.
                        The mean buttons
  of approaching headlights
  change into the always searching
  always aiming eyes of condors.
The lashing rainfall wails
  in Arabic for this Guernica
  in Beirut . . .
                        I think of Lorca
  who believed the lightning-worlds
  of love and poetry could have
  no enemies.
                        He never dreamed
  of lightning-chevrons on black
  shirts, lightning-wars
  and lightning-zigzags crayoned
  on a map that named a war

that scarred a generation . . .
This
generation's condors storm another
Spain.
The rain's a litany
of Lorcas bulldozed into pits.
The voice from Washington is no one's
and the world's.
Viva la Muerte!

THE DRENCHING

Targeted, I know that I can die
by lightning now.
Or now.
Or now.
I slog beneath the enfilade
of burst on burst of buckshot
rivers, lakes, oceans, cesspools
sunsucked to the clouds and spattered
back.
Puddles dance in rainfire.
Hopscotching, hurdling, wirewalking,
I slip the deeper pools
before I shrug it all to hell
and splatter straight ahead
like infantry.
Across the street
a girl has shucked her shoes.
She wades duck-happy in the sluice
of sewers.
Her skirt shapes
to her hips.
Her sweater defines
what sweaters define, but rainfully
moreso.
Laughing, she waves
at gawkers in a bus.

I half-expect
to hear, "Come in, the water's
fine."
Rainleaks start saucing
in my shoes.
Taxis go aquaplaning
by before a double spume
of spray.
The skyroof cracks
with skyflash, mends and cracks
again.
Hatcheted by wind,
a weeping willow splits
and splinters by a fountain brimmed
to flood by the real thing . . .
Socks oozing, suit
dripping (but not quite dry
as advertised), I'm in my element.
Lightning can smash.
The bilging sky
can spill from here to Mars,
and I'll still balk at doorway-docks
and awning-harbors.
Rainlocked,
I'm free of how my clothes
presented me.
But still I'm stuck
with them, and still they drag
me down.
By the waters of Babylon
Boulevard, I bear them like a cross
beneath a kingdom come
of thunder.
A bus maneuvers
like an ark adrift with prisoners.
She of the sculpting sweater
saunters in gutterwater.
A boy in overalls wades by,
licking his strawberry cone
as if nothing's happening.

ONLY THE NEW BRANCHES BLOOM

For Grace, July 19, 1978

Denying what it means to doubt,
this year's forsythias unfold
and flood the air with yellow
answers.
They say it's time
I opened up, time I learned
French, time I liked less
and loved more, time
I listened to the sun, time
I made time.
Why not?
Can days of making sense
of days that make no sense
make sense?
If nothing's sure
but nothing's sure, then reading
Montesquieu must wait.
Preparing for my enemies must
wait.
And gravity the hurrier
must wait because forsythias
are happening.
They make me
turn my back on facts,
insurance policies, inoculations.
wire barbed or braided,
bodyguards and all the folderol
of fear.
They say that this
year's blossoms will outlive
the lasting death of Mars.
There are no flowers on the stars.

CHILD OF OUR BODIES

Midway to birth, you are your own
secret. No one can tell me
how you'll be or when or where . . .

Not that the universe will change.
Suspended in the wombing air
where everything begins, the earth

keeps rolling on its ring from sun
to moon to sun again. I've sailed
the circle almost forty times,

but now your future makes me live
a different present than the one
I lived before you happened. Yes,

happened! After eleven years
my only precedent is silence.
I wait the justice of your eyes

exactly as I'm waiting now
for words to say what waiting means.
It does no good to school myself

for possibilities. Between
what never was and what shall be,
the only bravery is innocence.

TO MY MOTHER

Had you survived that August afternoon
of sedatives, you would be sixty-three,
and I would not be rummaging for words
to plot or rhyme what I would speak to you.

Tonight I found a diary you kept
in 1928, and while I read
your script in English, Arabic and Greek,
I grudged those perished years and nearly wept

and cursed whatever god I often curse
because I scarcely knew one day with you
or heard you sing or call me by my name.
I know you were a teacher and a nurse

and sang at all the summer festivals.
You made one scratched recording of a song
I often play when no one else is home,
but that is all I have to keep you real.

The rest exists in fragile photographs,
a sudden memoir in my father's eyes
and all the anecdotes of thirty years
remembered like a portrait torn in half

and torn in half again until a word
deciphered in a diary rejoins
these tatters in my mind to form your face
as magically as music overheard

can summon and assemble everything
about a day we thought forever past.
For one recovered second you are near.
I almost hear you call to me and sing

before the world recoils and returns . . .
I have no monument, my beautiful,
to offer you except these patterned lines.
They cannot sound the silentness that burns

and burns although I try to say at last
there lives beyond this treachery of words
your life in me anew and in that peace
where nothing is to come and nothing past.

SILENCE SPOKEN HERE

What absence only can create
needs absence to create it.
Split by deaths or distances,
we all survive like exiles
from the time at hand, living
where love leads us for love's
reasons.
We tell ourselves
that life, if anywhere, is there.
Why isn't it?
What keeps us
hostages to elsewhere?
The dead
possess us when they choose.
The far stay nearer than we know
they are.
We taste the way
they talk, remember everything
they've yet to tell us, dream
them home and young again
from countries they will never leave.
With friends it's worse and better.
Together, we regret the times
we were apart.
Apart, we're
more together than we are
together.
We say that losing
those we love to living
is the price of loving.
We say
such truthful lies because
we must—because we have
no choices.
Face to face
we say them, but our eyes
have different voices.

MAPS FOR A SON ARE DRAWN AS YOU GO

I say what Lindbergh's father
said to Lindbergh: "One boy's
a boy; two boys are half
a boy; three boys are no
boy at all."
Which helps explain
why Lindbergh kept his boyishness
for life, which meant he stayed
himself, which means a lot.
What else is destiny?
After
you learn that governments lie
and happiness is undefinable
and death has no patience,
you'll understand me.
Meanwhile
the ignorant but well informed
will try to keep you mute
as a shut book.
Forecasters of the best
and worst will hurry to retreat
infallibly into the future.
Ministers
who talk on cue with God
will weigh you down like serious
furniture.
Assume that what
you lose to such distractions
you will gain in strength.
By then you'll learn that all
you know will help you less
than how you think.
The rest

is memory, and memory's the graveyard
of the mind as surely as tomorrow
is its myth.
Nowhere but the time
at hand is when you'll see
that God's geometry is feast
enough.
Within the world's
closed circles, everything's
the sum of halves that rhyme.
From coconuts to butterflies
to lovers knotted on the soft
battlefield of any bed, the halves
add up to one, and every
one remembers where it came
from as a trumpet note
recalls the song it was a part of
and the listeners who heard it
and were changed.
What Lindbergh's
father meant and what I mean
are two roads to the same
country.
Knowing how long
it takes us to be young, he left
his son some clues to get
his bearings by.
And so do I.

JOSEPH AWAD

(1929–)

Joseph Awad

Joseph Awad was born in Shenandoah, Pennsylvania, in 1929. His family moved to Washington, D.C., in 1939, where he graduated from Georgetown University. He did graduate work in English at George Washington University and attended the Corcoran School of Art.

Awad joined Reynolds Metals Company in 1957 and serves as corporate director of public relations. He is a vice-president and member of the board of the Reynolds Metals Foundation. In 1982 he served as national president of the Public Relations Society of America and was awarded the Thomas Jefferson Award for career achievements by the society's Old Dominion Chapter. His book *The Power of Public Relations* was published in 1985 by Praeger Publishers, New York.

Since 1963, Awad and his wife, Doris, with their ten children, have lived in Richmond, Virginia. He serves on the board of trustees of the *New Virginia Review*.

Awad's poetry has been published in such periodicals as *America*, *Commonweal*, the *Kansas Quarterly*, the *William & Mary Review*, *Parnassus*, and others. He has had poems included in the 1980, 1981, 1985, and 1987 editions of Alan Pater's *Anthology of Magazine Verse and Yearbook of American Poetry*. His book of poems, *The Neon Distances*, was published in 1980 by Golden Quill Press.

Karla Hammond, in her review in the *Small Pond Magazine*, wrote of *The Neon Distances*: "His is a style distinctively singular even when he borrows or free associates. . . A wisdom startling in its simplicity."

"Obsession or Grace"

A friend, writing about my work in the Georgetown Journal *years ago, commented that my mixture of Arab and Irish blood was a sure recipe for a poet. I do think I was born at least in the foothills of Parnassus. As a child I wanted to be an artist. Then I fell in love with reading. I wrote my first poems at age thirteen or fourteen, fired up, as I remember, by my first reading of some of Keats' poetry. I've since given a great part of my days and nights (especially nights) to trying to make words into . . . what? Not verbal constructs, but what Horace described as "complete organisms that give their own special kind of pleasure." Why do I continue writing poems? Because I have to. Is it an obsession? Or is it a grace?*

It was not until quite recently that I ever thought of myself as an Arab American, though I have always cherished my Lebanese heritage. My paternal grandparents came to America around the turn of the century from a town near Beirut. Because of my mother's illness and early death, as a child I went to live with Sithee. She spoke Arabic (especially when excited) and I understood what she was saying. To my regret, I never learned Arabic, though I well remember the names of all her heavenly Lebanese dishes.

I have kept my career as a corporate public relations professional separate and apart from my vocation as poet. I must confess I find it irritating that today "serious poetry" is deemed almost the exclusive preserve of academicians. Some people feel that a businessman, particularly a "corporate type," cannot possibly be more than a casual versifier. I take courage from the precedent of Wallace Stevens.

Unfortunately, while poetry seems to make up a sizeable subculture in American society, it is not a major force in the general culture. This may be due in part to poets. As Aristotle wrote, the greatest virtue of diction is to be clear without being commonplace. The best poetry ignites the spirit and illuminates, like sunlight, a world of imaginative experience. Poetry must be written with respect, even love, for the reader. This implies respect, even love, for language and its conventions. While I enjoy all kinds of poetry, my preference is for poetry powerfully felt, fashioned with conscious artistry.

THE MAN WHO LOVED FLAMENCO

Andalusia—in the rolling of its saying
You could taste already
The black wine lolling on your tongue.
It made you heady
like the gypsy ballads of Garcia Lorca,
Cannonades of classical guitars,
The brazen pomp and trumpets of the bullfight,
Your dreamed sierras under the lost stars.

You applauded, stomped, you yelled *ole*,
When the dancers' high heels drilled out dots and dashes—
Innuendoes, dangers, diablos only you could decipher—
Camellias in the midnight hair, eyes flashing,
Skirts whirling, storms of thundering guitars,
The anguish, the rapture of the singers,
The fire, the scorn, the high-chinned arrogance,
The clicking of the ringed and lifted fingers.

Once, when we were students burning
With sangria and a time in bloom,
Carried away by the music, the rush of the rhythm,
You jumped up in the living room,
Clapping your hands above your head, looking
At your heels with lowered eyelids. With no care
For your gimpy leg, you who walked with a limp,
You who repose in a quiet grave somewhere,
Danced with the daring of an Escudero.

A LAMENT FOR PHILIP LARKIN

Farewell, Phyllyp, adew!
Our Lorde thy soul reskew!
—John Skelton, *Phyllyp Sparowe*

Philip, your poems tell. It was your lot
To be the losers' laureate, to sing
The secular emptiness, the license loosed
By diaphragm and pill, deception's knot,
Greenery receding, those who wake
In mill towns on dark mornings and who dream
Of shouting, "Stuff your pension," who endure
The rue, the boredom of the beds they make.
Cranky librarian! Crafty recluse!
You braved the loveless nights with jazz and books.
The language was your girl. You liked her tough
Yet tender to the sadness of your muse.
Yours was a "rough-tongued" art. You lived apart
From posturing poets. Merciless, you mapped
The pomp, the pathos of our Whitsun weddings
From a passing railcar window of the heart.
A metaphor for faith beyond recapture,
Beyond regret, you dared in "The High Windows."
Sun-comprehending glass—it lifts
Despair to the half-hope of prayerful rapture.
In quiet churches, harbored from the din,
You surprised a hunger to be serious
That "someone will forever be surprising."
Like a ruffled sparrow by a lovelit window,
You sang for a bleak season, looking in.

I THINK CONTINUALLY OF THOSE WHO WERE TRULY FAILURES

I think continually of those who were truly great . . .
—Stephen Spender

I think continually of those who were truly failures,
Who, from the womb, dragged irrelevant regret
Down shuttered streets and brooded over polls
Indifferent to their own unfriendly faces;
Whose broken hopes came poking through the elbows
Of shabby ways they saw no sense in mending;
Who might at most have salvaged from the curb
The butt ends of discarded martyrdoms.

What is unendurable is to thrive
Beyond a love the soul was never up to,
Or a hate not sharp enough to kill;
To have felt the spark's pinch, winced at stars,
And not have cared much one way or another;
To have been locked out all night on moonless steps
And never the least anxious for the dawn.

In bars, in the cracked corridors of old office buildings,
See how their dust seeks out the darker corners,
Who lived lagging behind their hopes,
Unfurling the pale, bravado smile
Of those who surrender without a fight.
Born of defeat, stood up by every dream but death,
They hung around for awhile and left
Walls of graffiti signed with their dishonour.

GENERATIONS

See how he loves me.
Sunlight racing
Down the front porch steps,
He flies into my arms,
Engulfing me like summer.
In a small boy's eyes—joy,
A joy I father.
His head nests on my shoulder,
Dusksoft,
Darkening my vision.
I would die for him.
He hangs on tight
As if I might.

FIRST SNOW

Parents far asleep in the next room,
The boy creeps out from high-piled quilt and blankets,
Vamped by a ghostly silver window light.
Cheek against the icy glass, he gawks
At white from nowhere filling all the night—
The streets, the roofs of porches, the black trees—
A living white, alive with minute winks
And sparkles, wheeling endlessly
In the widening silence; not a sound to start
The spirit from its perfect wonder. (Wonder
Is praise unspoken.)

Now they are far asleep in frozen hills.
There have been blazing summers, a great war.
And all the skylines of his world have changed.
Cheek once more against a winter window,
He wonders at the silent white descent,
Wife asleep in the room, the children grown

And roaming skylines of their own tonight
(Be with them, Lord). It is as if no years
Or war or neon din had intervened,
As if the boy had never left the window,
As I watch the snow falling forever in the darkness
Like visible love.

THE WIDOWER

Whatever it was is lost to memory.
Something I did or something that wasn't done
In the running world of first or second grade
Meant that my father had to see the nun.
We hiked the long blocks in the morning chill,
Down Chestnut Street, past the darkened Strand,
Up the wind-blown hill. No word was said.
All the way to school he held my hand.
How it all turned out is lost to memory.
The grip of his hand. The bite of his wedding band.

AUTUMNAL

Death, it is all about us lately.
Uncle Joe buried just three weeks.
Now uncle Leo gone. And Richard gone.
It is the season. The insistent years.
Like winds that strip away the leaves,
Wear us down, resigned to go more gentle.
Even the hidden how, the grim unknown
Of hour or place, wakefulness or pain,
Intimidate us less each autumn. Now
Disquiet whispers with a deeper question;
Whether, before the frost, we will have done
Whatever the work we were created for?
Was it for one, supreme, heroic deed,
Pivotal, that might reshape the world?
Or the accumulating labors, day by day,

That make an exemplary life? Perhaps
My *raison d'etre* is given in this instant—
Looking up to see you enter smiling,
Leaning, in autumn roselight from the window,
To put your hand upon my drooping shoulder.
Is it the knowing I alone was born—
Of all Arabia's lovers, I alone—
To sing the secret of this living moment
That fills my windswept spirit with such peace,
And so much praise?

FOR JUDE'S LEBANON

It is said he was a relative of Jesus,
That his apostolate
Was to the land we know as Lebanon,
That he gave his blood for Christ.
What wonders did he perform
To win the Barnum & Bailey blurb,
"Patron saint of the impossible."

I'm beginning a novena to St. Jude.

His lone epistle opens lovingly:
"Jude, the servant of Jesus Christ
And brother of James, to the called
Who have been loved in God the Father
And preserved for Christ Jesus,
Mercy and peace and love
Be yours in abundance."

I'm beginning a novena to St. Jude.

He had a poet's way with words.
Evil, sensual men he called
"Wild waves of the sea,
Foaming up their shame,
Wandering stars for whom

The storm of darkness
Has been reserved forever."

I'm beginning a novena to St. Jude.

In Lebanon there is loud lamentation.
Beirut, once beautiful Beirut,
Bloodied by Christian, Jew and Druze,
Weeps like a wound just under the world's heart.
Pontius Pilates in world capitals
Wash their hands, pronouncing solemnly,
"The situation is impossible."

I'm beginning a novena to St. Jude.

STOPPING AT THE MAYFLOWER

Father, your hallowed ghost
Will always haunt me here. The old hotel
Is being renovated. In the ballrooms
Moldings and golden bas-reliefs
Have been restored to their original splendor.
(If only they could restore that golden grin.)
And so this morning, early,
I descended the dim staircase off the lobby
To see the barber shop before it's shorn
Of my particular memories, redone
Beyond our time together. Your poet son
Climbed the shoe shine stand, unrecognized
By the aging man who worked there in his prime
When you were manager. He could not know
His busy presence brought me close to you.

I could see, inside the shop, the barber chair
You worked from eight to six, six days a week.
I thought of my Georgetown years, lost afternoons
When I dropped by near quitting time. I'd peruse
The old *Times-Herald* or *The Daily News*

Until you finished your last customer,
Who, introduced, would say, as if on cue,
"Your dad is very proud of you."

You would clip and cut my hair, shave my neck,
Give me a shampoo and a steaming towel,
Order me a shine. "The works," you'd quip,
Treating me better than your biggest tipper.
I'd wait while you checked out the register
As I did long years before in Shenandoah.
(We lived behind the shop then. I'd rush in
On Saturday, your busiest day, demanding
In front of all your grinning customers,
A quarter for the movies . . . and some candy.)

As the old man brushed and buffed my shoes
I stared hard at your empty chair.
For an instant you were standing there
In your white tunic, shaking out the hair
From a barber cloth and calling, "Next."
Spying me, you smiled, father-wise,
Lighting the Lebanese midnight of your eyes.

The shine was finished now. The man was waiting.
(I remembered Shenandoah long ago.
The morning of mother's funeral we walked uptown
Dressed in Sunday suits and new black ties.
You bought us both a shine.) With hurting eyes
And heart, I went up to the lobby, found the doors.

You would hardly know Connecticut Avenue.
New buildings have crowded out the old.
Your favorite restaurant's gone. The wind was cold.
I walked the block or so to the cathedral
Where you went to Mass before or after work
Or during lunch on holy days. Before
The altar of our God (my faith in Him
Your precious gift to me) I prayed for you,
Remembering a dream I had one night

Shortly after you died. You were in the shop
In Shenandoah, busy at your chair,
Honing your razor on the leather strop,
Preparing to shave a customer tilted back,
Reclining corpse-like under the white cloth.
The customer lifted his head.
It was Jesus and, accusing me
With eyes that pierced me through, he said,
"Your dad is very proud of you."

VARIATIONS ON A THEME

Sculpture, heroic as it is, over the ages
Is doomed to lose a nose or a marble arm.
When the great library burned at Alexandria,
The certain fame of emperors and poets
Was combusted in smoke and popping sparks.
I can remember when the whole world trembled
To *Sieg Heils* thundered round a paperhanger.
More recently all that's left of Howard Hughes
And J. Paul Getty and their fabled billions
Are tabloid blurbs. Holes in the skull tell only
That kissable lips and arch brown eyes are gone.
That is why, looking down on all this dazzle
From the top of the World Trade Center—dazzle
That, a dream from now, will be an obscure legend,
And mostly disbelieved—I make this note:
Tell her you love her.

EUGENE PAUL NASSAR

(1935–)

Eugene Paul Nassar

Most people of Eugene Paul Nassar's accomplishments leave the small towns or cities of their birth—Nassar did not. Born in Utica, New York, in 1935, he traveled for education, receiving his B.A., M.A., and Ph.D. from Kenyon College, Oxford University and Cornell University, respectively. But Utica had its hold on him, and it is the Lebanese-American life there of the forties and fifties that he celebrates with the eye of one who belongs.

Nassar's collection of prose poems, *Wind of the Land*, was published in 1979 by the Association of Arab American University Graduates (AAUG). It is now available from the Ethnic Heritage Studies Center, Utica College of Syracuse University, Utica, New York 13502 (where Dr. Nassar teaches). About *Wind of the Land*, Dr. Evelyn Shakir wrote in *Ethnic Forum* (1983): "[It] is a treasure trove of Arab folklore, which is fast disappearing, one suspects, even in Lebanon itself. And it is certainly the closest thing we have to a narrative defining the second-generation of Arab-American experience and thus rescuing it from possible oblivion."

A respected literary critic himself, Nassar has published *Wallace Stevens: An Anatomy of Figuration* (University of Pennsylvania Press, 1965); *The Cantos of Ezra Pound* (John Hopkins University Press, 1975); and *Essays: Critical and Metacritical* (Fairleigh Dickinson University Press, 1983), among other works.

Nassar is married and has three children.

"The Rarest of Wines"

My writing in literary scholarship has been largely in the close analysis and explication of difficult texts of modern American poetry: the poems of Wallace Stevens, Hart Crane, and Ezra Pound. I have tried also to speak precisely about the poetry of Kahlil Gibran as a Lebanese-American emigre poet (in MELUS, 7:2, reprinted in my Essays: Critical and Metacritical*). In my memoir of growing up Lebanese-American in the Italian-American neighborhood of East Utica in upstate New York, I try in two prose-poems, "East Utica" and "Disputation with Kahlil Gibran," to evoke the rich, often joyful, often sad, experience of the second-generation immigrant's child, to detail a social ethos full of humor, pathos, and sentiment. The peasant Arabic dialect of my parents' generation, with its exquisite ironies, has always delighted me. Their stories, their values, and the immense vitality in their storytelling, is the rarest of wines to me, and is a vintage which is passing away. I have tried to fix their era and that of my childhood and youth in a memoir which might prevail somewhat against time, the particular enemy of all non-mainstream social contexts.*

From EAST UTICA

Lebanon, land of our birth and hopefully of our dying,
We, thy exiled sons, are disgraced in the foreign land,
Confined we are by the oppressor,
The sun and wind are denied us,
Also our game of pinochle.
   oof! (says the audience)

oof, oof, oo oo oo oo oo oof! (says Abdullah, meditating)

Here is your child Mike, who lolled in the vineyards of Zahle,
Who saw from his window the Mount of Sunnin,
His wife, a princess without question,
   Mintaha of the Wadi,

Lies in a lonely bed,
Her darling is missing.
  oof!

oof, oof! oo oo oo oo oo oo oo oo oo oo oof!

See here your youngest child, Aid, mender of shoes,
Is suffering perhaps from constipation.
The young man is in need of the cool spring water,
Only the streams of Beirut
Will purge those little devils.
  oof!

  oof, oof.

St. Maron, protect us from our humorless oppressors
Who don't know veal from mutton,
Forgive us, poor wayfarers,
Who left the meaningful, the holy land,
And play cards in our old age.
  oof.

oof, oof.

Forgive old Joe here, who eats sweets by the bushel,
He has forgotten the old country delicacies.
We wonder that he can eat American candy
Who has in the nostrils of his mind
Khreibe, Bitlawa, and the buttered ladyfingers.

  oof!

  oo oo oo oo oof!

Here in this land of debasement, O Virgin
  Mother, the moon rules the sun.
The women have strings around the men's testicles,
The child punishes the father,
And the God-fearing Lebanese is forced from his family

Without coffee or a cigar.
  oof!
  oof!

See Abe here, whose mustache is quivering with rage,
And Khalil, whose eyes are closing with grief,
Honorable men must give their trousers to scoundrels,
The mouse is asked to ride on the camel's back.
  oof!

oof oof oof oof! oo oo oo oo oo oo—f!

Praise be to the Lord then for the Coffee-House,
Refuge of the saintly and the sons of the mountain,
Praised be the heart that still feels, Man for Man,
Son for mother, child for grandfather, cousin for cousin.
  oof!

And thank the Lord for the spirit that burns,
In exile and in prison, among charlatans and fools,
To die with nothing to be ashamed of, with your trousers on,
Your wife at home, and good cards in your hand.

Yu, Yu, Yu, Yu, Yu, Yu, Yu!

From A DISPUTATION WITH KAHLIL GIBRAN

The Arab woman is wailing in the parlor.
Our parlor is not of the newest style.
I can barely hear the woman's voice from the bedroom.
She sings of a lost lover beneath the rubble on the record.
It is as if she is alive and singing in a deep past that I
Have just managed to reach.
The young Arabs tell me she is not of the newest style.
My bedroom is very narrow,
All the walls of the house are crooked,
And our yard outside will win no prizes despite my loving it.

The woman's voice is almost all that is necessary
To put me on the hill with Abraham
Or down with Plato in the shade.
Her voice is like a clothespin on a clothesline.

*

Father Bschara, visiting the sick at the hospital in the Twenties of this century, knowing little English, so speaking Arabic, sprinkling Catholic, Protestant, Jew, willy nilly, enjoying himself. And into the room of Ameen, one of his parishioners, stone-deaf:

"Ya Uncle Ameen, how are you today? May the good Lord take you by nightfall."

"Thank you, Father Bschara, bless your lips."

"Then, my Cousin, we will bury you three days from now."

"May it be as you say, if God wills, Uncle."

"You will certainly be damned with the devils."

"With your prayers, dear Brother."

A very religious story, depending on one's world.

One's context, my friend Gibran, one's center, one's place, one's tradition.

You who spurn the walls of one's house and hunt vaporous birds, come and be one of us.

Do not seek to put man in a cosmic dimension, but to humanize the cosmos, for there surely is laughter, and strength against tragedy.

The page sings to the one who knows what it is to talk to birds on wires, and who has listened to the troubles of the nut and bolt.

*

Clothespins on a clothesline, back to the Wadi, back to Abraham, back deep in a human heart. The garden in front of your eyes shimmering. Veins of lettuce leaf flowing into the heart of the Lord. Dogs shagging about the neighborhood, talking to ladies. Night visions under the moon in valleys. One's world.

And the bird has built a nest in the fender of my brother's car. Most likely the same bird.

The same bird that perches so nicely on corners of buildings we can see, and who bends the branches, sings in the shade of our pear tree, and basks each summer on a tomato stick. The same, or very like.

*

If one has the love
The flower by the wall
Is more than wallflower in a windy world.
If one has the love
The flower blushes to a sisterly rose
And bids you, brother, come
Into her spacious sunlit garden.
But only if one has the love.

*

Once the muscatel grape is pressed and the ten-day wine ready, the copper still, the *karaki*, is cleaned and rinsed (five gallon this house, fifty gallon that house), the Lebanese in America attempt to equal the arak of the old country: the wine boiled on the stove, the vapors caught in the copper coils bent into the garbage can of flowing water. The distillate, the white wine alcohol, gathered to 80 proof, by taste or hygrometer, and returned to the karaki, and the anise seed, the *yansoon*, added one pound to the gallon; the mixture distilled, gathered to 150 proof, or till the drops come milky from the coil, later cut to 120 proof with spring water, the arak ready.

*

Can you not see that you will not satisfy man, Kahlil Gibran, with your cold abstractions of Love and Life beyond the personal love and life, with your Great Soul or Great Self, or Vast Man or Master Spirit? We have had it all before (postcards to Blake and Whitman). Man will have his Heaven with private rooms and his personal immortality with his shoes on.

You do him wrong to turn him from his village or his village culture. But you know this, my brother, my countryman. Is there any village more beautiful than Bscharri, your village?

*

Your children are not your children. O my Gibran, have you ever made a greater miscalculation? No village rebel ever made a greater. *You may strive to be like them, but seek not to make them like you.* O my God, worse and worse! Watch out for Shafee'a, Kahlil, she will eat you alive! And Abdullah will expose your weaknesses to laughter.

*

"He's a smart guy, this tree. He gives apples one year and he takes it easy one year. He says 'If I come too much, just like relatives, you may use me poorly. If you wait for me, you will treat me well.' "

"Now you peach tree, you young whelp, listen to my words. Your father, Michael Nassar here of Zahle and I have been bringing you up for eleven years and you have given us nothing. Now act like a man and give us some big delicious peaches right away."

"Ya Mike, our uncle the pear has been giving rich beautiful fruit without a spot for the thirty-three years we have been married. And all we do for him is bless him and fill the bushels. And the plum next to him is weak and we take the worms from his roots every year and he does not recover."

"Ya Mintaha, some bear and some do not bear; some live long and well, and some are weak and die quick. Nobody knows what is in the mind of the good God."

"Ya Mike, do you remember the great mulberry tree by your uncle's house in the Wadi? How we would all sit in it and eat and eat."

"I remember my Uncle Paul shouting to you in his loud voice 'Ya, Mintaha of the House of Kassouf, if you continue to eat of our Mulberry, you will have the blood of the Nassars in you and then you will have to marry Mike when you get older and make the graft complete!' And I said 'No, Uncle Paul, the Kassoufs have an Apricot, and you can't graft an apricot to a mulberry.' "

"And what do you now say, ya Mike?"

*

Grapes from the central market, grapes from the street corners, storefronts of East Utica, zinfandel and muscatel in the October air, wine barrels washed and charred with candle flame, cellars fragrant with fermenting juice. Three days with skins, stems, and seeds, the first juice poured through funnel into barrel, mash remaining in the cradle sticks of the wine press. The arm of the press turned one notch, and the half-hour wait till the turn to another notch, the pressed juice running, dribbling, then dripping down the lip of the press into the waiting cask; daydreaming by the furnace, chair tipped back, spider in the corner weaving. Three days to fill the two fifty-gallon barrels, then months of the juice alive in the slow final fermentation through winter, the unready Christmas wine, the racking at Easter time, the summer mellowing; the drinking at table and beneath the vine in the neighborhood yards, awaiting the coming grapes in the central markets and at the street corners, store fronts down the street, down the corners of East Utica.

*

"Ma, this is Kahlil Gibran's famous book of poetry, he is a Lebanese writer from Bscharri, above the holy Wadi Qadischa."

"But my son, why all these pictures of men and women without pants?"

"Ya Auntie, how do you like our new wallpaper?"

"The wall is fine, but why that picture of that old whore on the wall? Put up a nice picture of some saint."

"Beauty is spring water gushing from the rock," says Yusef Elasmar, "and the good man's thirst quenched." "The apricot in flower and the wind through it," says my father. "A young girl's pomegranate cheeks and almond eyes, that's what beauty is," says Abdullah. "The *Quoddous* of the mass," said Father Bschara long ago, "I can never keep from crying:

Quoddous, quoddous, quoddous,
Rabbou Sabaouth
Assama wul ard memlouatanee
min majdeka latheem.

[Holy, holy, holy, Lord God Almighty,
Heaven and Earth are full of your Glory.]

*

Beauty you say is in the ecstatic moment of a cosmic consciousness, of an awareness of the full potential of evolving greater man. I doubt, Gibran, that man will get any better than, say, Christ or Confucius. Or art any better than, say, Homer or Dante.

You spurn the here and the Hereafter, both at the root of the human heart, and offer us the *Übermensch* treading over our bones.

*

Why this exultation in the contraries of life, Gibran, in Good and Evil as One, Life and Death as One, the Darkness as blessed as Light? Is it not simply an avoidance of the fact of death, evil and darkness?

Is it not better to call the tragic tragic? and, if one is lucky, to embrace the transcendental Paradise, as with Dante, as with Abraham?

Even, if one is not lucky, to exult in the worlds, the continuities of those who can so embrace, as Bschara, as M'Boraky, as your people, my people?

*

He had walked in the rain and had lain on the bed. He awoke in the middle of the night and could hear water dripping from the gutters on the roof. The rain had finished. He heard a train whistle and the rolling of the freight cars. He loved these sounds. He got up and went out onto the porch.

It was a dripping, gorgeous night. There was no movement save water splish, splashing from leaf to leaf, rolling down the trunk of the apple tree and into the grass beneath. The road glistened, the bushes and the roses were beaded with drops of light. Plink, plank, gathered the pools, and the tree ached with water it would give to the ground. A shudder of wind lifted the leaves and brought them delicately back, and the water fell.

There was no time to beauty like this . . .

*

"And over there," said my great Uncle during my visit to Lebanon in the Summer of 1960, "is the burial place of Noah, whom the Lord spared when He brought down the rains for forty days on the world. Only half of him is there, from the belt down. He was very tall, as long as two horses. The other half of him is in Saidanaya, I think."

"But Noah was *Yahud*, isn't that so, Uncle? What's a Jew doing with half of him in Lebanon and half in Syria?"

"Those were the days, young joy of my eyes, when all people were together, praying to the one Lord, before everybody got split apart."

"Why then, Uncle, is poor Noah split in two?"

"I don't know if it is true, but my grandfather used to say that the Melkites were jealous we had the Saint in a Maronite village and came at night like devils and took half of him to Saidanaya."

*

Let's get down to it, Cousin Kahlil, Art mythologizes Life, but what life? Is it better to see Man in the image of a tree, as you do, or a tree in the image of a man, as I do? I think the latter. Nature is no resting place for man.

One had better turn to bless the deeply human, the local, the living past beneath the rubble of History.

Your moments are not my moments, O human brother, and your visions give me no serenity.

Your Presences are not my Presences.

*

The roses are full, full
The roses are always on my mind.
I love the roses only,
And, O my soul, the lettuce leaf.

—Lebanese folk song

*

Where is the America of our dreams, O brothers of my generation?
And the America of your dreams, O children of my brothers?
Where it always was, O brothers, in the hearts of our fathers,
In the acts of the good man who looks to his children,
In the joy of the child in the lap of his grandmother.
Filiality is the base of all good dreams.

America has indeed been lavish in the casting of flowers,
Of flowers that do not grow in the old country villages,
Generous, open, accessible in the highest of glories.
But what of the flowers, the country flowers of the village,
Simplicity, serenity, and joy, the sense of belonging?

Out of the tomb came Lazarus; out of our sometime
loneliness, O brothers,
Come the memories of a past that was not lonely,
And O my children, of an ethical life and a loyalty
That can withstand the assaults of the rational life.
Skepticism turns the ground, but bears no fruit of its own;
The seed is in the good love for each other.

And there is no love of the world without the love of your fathers,
No love of Man and the Universe without the love of your neighbors.
And a young man has been reading to me the poetry of Kahlil
Gibran
And wise he is in many things, O my children, and schooled in
sound,
But his is not the needful poetry, O my cousins,
For he is too lonely and would make a blessing of loneliness.

I say to my brother Gibran in his own words,
Come and be one of us.
Descend and appease your hunger with our bread,
And quench your thirst with our wine.
Our bread is in the tales of our grandmother and the wisdom
from her lips.
Our wine in the pomegranate cheeks and the gentleness of roses
in our wives.
The sanctity of our mothers in the whiteness of orange blossoms,
And our sisters' strength in the hills and streams of Lebanon.

And do not fear, O Kahlil Gibran, that the village dream
will stifle our children.
You would have us break boundaries in an ever-widening circle.
But a dream of love must be at the center of each circle.
A point, a place, a home to which the skylark must return,

Deep in the heart where is the seed of the Lord,
Love that illumines the day and the night,
That waters the garden of the children and the garden of the blind.
With the joy in one's father and the kiss of one's child.
  SALAAM.

H. S. (SAM) HAMOD

(1936–)

H. S. (Sam) Hamod

Gary, Indiana—Sam Hamod's birthplace in 1936—is also the locus of a mosque built by Hamod's father, a Muslim imam and immigrant from Lebanon. The poet son followed in his footsteps after a career teaching at American universities. Sam Hamod was director of the Islamic Center, Washington, D.C., in the turbulent years of 1938–84, and was education advisor for the Embassy of Qatar.

Hamod received his doctorate from the University of Iowa's Writers Workshop and published the first of eight books of poetry in that area, about which he has said, "I have to thank the good earth of the Midwest for a way of knowing and feeling that can be found in no other part of America." Among his collections are *Dying with the Wrong Name: New and Selected Poems* (Anthe, 1980), *The Famous Boating Party* (Cedar Creek, 1970), and *The Holding Action* (Seamark Press, 1969). His poems have appeared in a number of anthologies, including *Traveling America* (Macmillan, 1978) and *Settling America* (Macmillan, 1974).

Hamod has two children and currently lives with his wife, Marianne, in Washington, D.C., where he runs the National Communications Institute.

"A Mixture of Sounds"

My poems are a mixture of sounds heard and unheard from my life—from the men who lived in my parents' hotel, to B. B. King and Muddy Waters, to early Arabic records and readings from the Holy Qur'an. They are often songs to the courage and foolishness our parents demonstrated by coming to America, and they tell of the comic and tragic lives they, and we, all live, each in our own way—and yet each a part of some larger "we" that we as Arabs participate in.

At times, I want to speak only of poems, not of "ethnic poems." But, in truth, our ethnicity helps shape the way we see and the way we write—so it is a part of what our poems are made of. But a poem cannot lean on its ethnicity in order to keep from falling—a poem must be a good poem on its own.

In truth, a poem, aside from love itself, is the most intimate form of communication. Often we can say more to one another in a poem than we can in other forms of speech. What is sad is that often we become so engrossed in our workaday life that we lose the urge to feel, to write, to grow.

LINES TO MY FATHER

(*On the Death of My Father, Gary, Indiana, 1967*)

My Father is watching over his mosque, silently
He hovers now, praying;
My Father is sitting on the step watching,
Holding his chest where the bullet entered his prayer;
Holding on, the maple trees blurring in his eyes,
He cannot rise, he is praying as his blood comes,
My Father is planting maple trees beside his mosque,
   digging each hole
Carefully, patiently, knowing the trees will grow,
He is watering the grass outside his mosque at 3 a.m.,
His work is done;   now my Father covers the grass with love.

My Father is moving East, to Lebanon, eating kib'be, his
Mother offering him grapes and shade,
He is walking in the mountains, drinking water;
My Father is sitting on a park bench beside me
Taking the air, watching my children in the grass,
He is talking of water,
Trying to rest,
But he must go   his mosque   waiting.
My Father, dreaming of water when wakened,
When I found him,   had only blood in his mouth.

1967–68

AFTER THE FUNERAL OF ASSAM HAMADY

(*For my mother, David and Laura*)

Cast:
Hajj Abbass Habhab: my grandfather
Sine Hussin: an old friend of my father
Hussein Hamod Subh: my Father
me

6 p.m.

middle of South Dakota
after a funeral in Sioux Falls
my father and grandfather
ministered the Muslim burial
of their old friend, Assam Hamady

me—driving the 1950 Lincoln
ninety miles an hour

"STOP! STOP!
stop this car!"

Why?
"STOP THIS CAR RIGHT NOW!"—Hajj Abbass
grabbing my arm from the back seat

"*Hysht Iyat*? (What're you yelling about?)"—my Father
"*Shu bikkee?*" (What's happening?)—Sine Hussin

I stop

"It's time to pray"—the Hajj
yanks his Navajo blanket
opening the door

"It's time to pray, *sullee*
the sun sets
time for *sullee*"

my Father and Sine Hussin follow
obedient
I'm sitting behind the wheel
watching, my motor still running

car lights scream by
more than I've ever seen in South Dakota

the Hajj spreads the blanket
blessing it as a prayer rug
they discuss which direction is East

after a few minutes it's decided
it must be that way
they face what must surely be South

they face their East, then notice
I'm not with them

"Hamode! get over here, to pray!"

No, I'll watch
and stand guard

"Guard from what—get over here!"

I get out of the car
but don't go to the blanket

My father says to the others:
"He's foolish, he doesn't know how
to pray."

they rub their hands
then their faces
rub their hands then
down their bodies
as if in ablution
their feet bare
together now
they begin singing
Three old men
chanting the Qur'an in the middle
of a South Dakota night

Allahu Ahkbar
Allahu Ahkbar

Ash haduu n lah illah illilawhh
Ash haduu n lah illah illilawhh

Muhammed rasoul illawh

in high strained voices they chant

Bismee lahee
a rah'manee raheem

more cars flash by

malik a youm a deen
ehde nuseerota el mustakeem
seyrota la theena

I'm embarrassed to be with them

en umta ailiy him
ghyrug mugthubee aliy him

people stream by, an old woman strains a gawk at them

willathouu leen—
Bismee lahee

I'm standing guard now

a rah'maneel raheem
khul hu wahu lahu uhud

They're chanting with more vigor now
against the cars—washing away
in a dry state
Hamady's death
he floats from their mouths
wrapped in white

Allahu sumud
lum yuulud wa'alum uulud

striped across his chest, with green

Walum yakun a kuf one uhud
willa thouu leen

his head in white, his grey mustache still

Ameen . . .

I hear them still singing
as I travel half-way across
America
to another job

burying my dead
I always liked trips, traveling at high speed
but they have surely passed me
as I am standing here now
trying so hard to join them
on that old prayer blanket—
as if the pain behind my eyes
could be absolution

1970

DYING WITH THE WRONG NAME
Three parts of an unfinished poem

(*Dedicated to all the immigrants who lost their names at Ellis Island*)

I.

These men died with the wrong names,
Na'aim Jazeeny, from the beautiful valley
of Jezzine, died as Nephew Sam,
Sine Hussin died without relatives and
because they cut away his last name
at Ellis Island, there was no way to trace
him back even to Lebanon, and Im'a Brahim
had no other name than mother of Brahim,
even my own father lost his, went from
Hussein Hamode Subh' to Sam Hamod.
There is something lost in the blood,
something lost down to the bone
in these small changes. A man in a
dark blue suit at Ellis Island says, with
tiredness and authority, "You only need two
names in America" and suddenly—as cleanly
as the air, you've lost
your name.   At first, it's hardly
even noticeable—and it's easier, you move

about as an American—but looking back
the loss of your name
cuts away some other part,
something unspeakable is lost.

And you know, these were not small
men, each was severe, though part
comic, as we will be remembered as well—but
Nephew Sam ran a cigar store in Michigan City, and
in the back room a poker game with chips and
bills often past 30,000; in his middle years,
Sine Hussin lifted the rear end of a 1939 Ford
so they could change a tire, and my father went
from Lebanon to the packinghouses in Sioux Falls
and Sioux City to the steel mills in Gary, from
nothing to houses and apartments worth more than
a million—in each sweaty day in Sioux City, down
to the boarding houses and small stores, in each drop
of movement at 5:30 and 5 a.m. cooking food for gandy
dancers and millworkers to nights working in the tavern
selling scotch while B. B. King and T. Bone Walker hustled
blues, each dollar another day mixing names and money.
And these were men who opened the world
with a gesture of the hand,
a nod and things moved, houses were built
for each new immigrant, apartment buildings bought
and sold—given as wedding presents
mayors and congressmen were made and broken—these men live
now on the edge of myth—each other under
a stone carved in English, the Arabic of Hussein Hamod Subh,
Na'aim Jazeeny, Sine Hussin
lost
each one sealed away
with the wrong name
except in this poem, and a poem
goes out to so few
but we trust as we can

II

Sine Hussin is still sitting in that
old chair, upholstered in brushed maroon wool,
he sits with his back to the window
at an angle, an old crystal lamp rests
on the ornate mahogany table, Im'a Brahim
sits in the companion chair, crocheting, her
legs full, veined and old, managing to walk, a
short osman of no more than 4'8" or so,
but obviously before her first child
the cameo shape of her face was more delicate, and
you know the smell of this room, meat and fried onions,
fresh garlic on the salad, tartness of lemon
twists into the air, and an ease toward evening
as you walk in
all the silence splits into hellos and hugs
while the world comes together
in the small room

III

Even now, it's hard for me to
fully understand what this old couple meant
to my father—
his own father had died before my father came
to America in 1914, his mother still in Lebanon,
unseen for decades. My father is 39 or 40 now, I
am 4 or 5, we are constantly carrying groceries
to this old house, the old couple always says "no"
but then they take them, but only after we have
some *fatiyah* and coffee, eat some fruit, talk
(I'm usually impatient to go), then we climb back
into the car and go home. My father, a man I came to know
as so secretive, yet so generous, a man alone; now I know
this was part of that other reality, where his name, that
language, Hussein, Sine Hussin, Im'a Brahim, *Asalamu Aleikum*,

all of these sounds were part of his name, this was that other
edge of Lebanon he carried with him, that home, that same
good food of the rich smells, it had to be in these moments,
these things
were not lost, but were alive and living in this room,
in this house, in these people, in this moment.

1978–79

LETTER

(for Sally)

The shaking in my hands
makes it hard
to write you
tell you of what's going on
inside—walls are light green
white
we go out for walks every
day, television's rationed, hard
rock, I sometimes remb—remember (the
lines come easier now, I forget about the
shaking when I'm talking to you) I
remember Jerry's hands
last Memorial Day
went down to his old print shop,
reached across his chest scratched
his shoulder, his hand just kept jumping
all over the place, he couldn't hold it down
I couldn't understand how it would feel, but I
have to hold on very tightly to my hands
or they'd talk all over the place
and you wouldn't be able to understand a word

1969

LEAVES

(for Sally)

Tonight, Sally and I are making stuffed
grapeleaves, we get out a package, it's
drying out, I've been saving it in the freezer, it's
one of the last things my father ever picked in this
life—they're over five years old
and up to now
we just kept finding packages of them in the
freezer, as if he were still picking them
somewhere packing them
carefully to send to us
making sure they didn't break into pieces.

* * *

"To my Dar Garnchildn
Davd and Lura
from Thr Jido"
twisted on tablet paper
between the lines
in this English lettering
hard for him even to print,
I keep this small torn record,
this piece of paper stays in the upstairs storage,
one of the few pieces of American
my father ever wrote. We find his Arabic letters
all over the place, even in the files we find
letters to him in English, one I found from Charles Atlas
telling him, in 1932,
"Of course, Mr. Hamod, you too can build
your muscles like mine . . . "

* * *

Last week my mother told me, when I was
asking why I became a poet, "But don't you remember,

your father made up poems, don't you remember him
singing in the car as we drove—those were poems."
Even now, at night, I sometimes
get out the Arabic grammar book
though it seems so late.

1973

LIBYAN/EGYPTIAN ACROBATS/ISRAELI AIR CIRCUS

(*February 21, 1973*)

the fighters come
from the left of the plane
I can see them,   they are to my right
I can see them
they come in from the left behind the tail
the first Phantom streaks in at 45 degrees
he's at 8 o'clock when he lets loose
his rockets flash forward
bang into the wing tank
wing explodes
it comes apart slowly in the air,
another explosion, the plane
is coming apart
the people, so small in the large sky,
are performing acrobatics
they tumble
carelessly through the sky
as if they are performing for the Israeli Air Circus
these dolls' arms come off as the planes strafe
the French pilot in the Libyan airliner is the only one
who can see where he's going
he's going down
into the hardness of desert sand

there is no Hebrew parallelism here
these are not simply eyes you take

1973

From MOVING

so we move now
my new wife and I, my children
move further away   like lost
shipmates crying to me for help
asking for some sound, some signal to understand
about this Arabic I sometimes speak   what Islam means to
  horizons
trying to grasp at these new patterns in the early morning darkness
floating out into the distance
and me their father—too far
away to be of much help
to be of any use
when they wake up afraid at night
wondering what that noise is
they wonder and wander without choice in this matter
it is when we are at sea this way
that I sometime think about a life
I've never known except for a little while
in some old country of time that I remember my father and
  grandfather
talking about, when I kept wanting to go out to play baseball,
a certain amount of a reality
where at least the whole tribe moved *together*
it was that way in my "old country" of
stories of truth my father and grandfather and their grandfather
  before them
everyone   everything stuck together   things stayed
and when they moved
grandfathers   grandmothers   fathers

mothers   children   grandchildren
moved together, in the tents, the whole world
moved in that tent
now
I carry no one in my tent.

JACK MARSHALL

(1937–)

Jack Marshall

Of Iraqi-Syrian-Jewish heritage, Jack Marshall was born in Brooklyn in 1937. His father, born in Baghdad in 1888, came to the United States in the 1920s after working at a fabric store in Manchester, England. It was in England that the family name changed from Mash^cal (or torch) to Marshall.

Typical of the multi-faith Syrian communities that traced themselves back to the very first Arab community in America—Washington Street, New York—garment making dominated Marshall's early life. He majored in literature at Brooklyn College at night while working in the family business by day, eventually leaving school to help his family full-time. Later, he set forth on a Norwegian freighter for Africa, returning to work in New York City as an advertising copywriter. He married the poet Kathleen Fraser in 1960, and the couple had a son.

Moving to San Francisco (his current home) in 1967, Marshall worked as a house painter, longshoreman, and manager of a clothing store. He has also taught at a number of universities, including the University of Iowa Writers Workshop.

Among his seven published books of poetry, the two most recent are *Arriving on the Playing Fields of Paradise* (Jazz Press, 1984), which won the Bay Area Book Reviewers Award for poetry, and *Arabian Nights* (Coffee House Press, 1986). In addition to prose works, Marshall has written a play about Shabbatai Zevi, the seventeenth-century Turkish Jew who proclaimed himself Messiah in 1648.

"To Create New Life"

My reason for writing—to create new life, or at least the possibility for it. I don't think of myself as either an Arab or Jewish poet; I just use the experience I have. My notion of poetry has boiled down to this: precise perception propelled. I am talking about it at its best, of course. I feel addressed by Wittgenstein's remark: "To create a language is to create a form of life."

THIRTY-SEVEN

Waking to find yourself the same
age your father was eight years before you
were born,
                    and already the massed weight of
your experience shakes you.
Tenderness gone, and longing,
                                        though you send it, unspent,
away, won't go.

Your son is somewhere else, so often
is he in your thoughts, and you doubt
he can know this.
Each time you see him feels like the first
                                                  and last.

Alone in your room,
what do you want of him
alone in his room?—absence
real as any event . . .
                              How being far
from that missed encounter diminishes, fills
you with a lack of,
the courage to care . . .

                              His is a childhood

Not yours, not nearly,
though you would wish it,
and if you were there,
would again be different.

Now, as when a boy, you fear
coming to nothing,
and under the eaves the owl hoots
from the night world still in sight
to a sun you woo, unrisen
unless you go down.

LETTER TO MY FATHER ON THE OTHER SIDE

Your nights draw nearer
as your face drifts away.
Though now the Atlantic Ocean stands
between us like frosted glass,
you were never closer . . .
not even when you approached
to offer me your failing business.

Success! You tried
but lacked the know-how.
Like a kept woman,
thankless, mean, insatiable,
it ate away your life
and what it left was not enough
to meet the sumptuous needs
extorted by the age.

It wasn't long before the squeeze
showed in your shuffling gait;
yet you stayed.
Watching you thin so,
I couldn't help quarreling
and soon left.
Yesterday, passing a dry-goods window

on the Rue St. Jacques,
with stockings much too long
for its plaster foot display
(toeless, just like yours),
brought it back to me:
the dim shop
on the ghost town's edge,
its cramped window dizzy
with Arabic-tipped lettering—
signs you stayed up nights
penning like a scribe—
and you, less lord than janitor,
absently dusting the stacks
of never-diminishing towels,
waiting for the rush.
Instead, stray bargain hunters
came now and then, blinking
like rats;
having no one else, you stayed.

Holding out is everything.
Early today I went back
to see what more I could recognize.
Standing there before the window,
I saw a face, peeled and shopworn
from being too long under the hot lamps,
peer back at me.
Seeing it made me want to write you
after these many years.
Have you taken a room in town yet,
or do you still lay a blanket out
beneath the counter every night?

THE UNITED WAY

photo—narrow, leonine, Hebraic, old
man's gentle, nearly feminine
smiling face, saying, "I don't know you
but I love you"—not anything you'd say,
                    yet something, the same
crease sea-weathered deep in the cheek, same

flint—
bright hint, part scrutiny, part
pity glistening the eye
when you would break into a smile, make me
look again and wonder: how, George,

this eerie likeness of you
found its way
twenty steel stories
above Embarcadero's smoked glass, flag-tier-
topped corporate towers, up
of all places, under the clock
on the sunlit lunchroom wall of
Cooley, Godward, Castro, Huddleson & Tatum,
Attorneys at Law. Here, a week into
reading proof and language—legalese—
leaves on the tongue a texture,
numb,
like wet cement. Now, through it, flash

Rezi, the years put in, now you receding
back in your reclining chair
those long August afternoons going
slowly rose, violet, wine-red
tincture in the sunsetting wave

suddenly evening, the airy
thinness we breathed
gaining volume, weight, we hardly
needing to speak . . .

As for talk of
poetry's luxury, necessity,
I see you amused, lean slant, mimic the rough
wry sound of those stern Maine lobstermen
standing knee-deep among their pots,
asking, "Much demand for it?"

How alive then
our laughter was indistinguishable from the light
of being here, necessity's
luxury, new as the taste of
water to one maddened with thirst,
hearing his leathery tongue strike
the roof of his mouth like a wooden clapper . . .
And we listen
when in a demotic more detailed
and deadly than ours, he speaks
words that, once said, set
in the bone. And laughter no water.

Each day earlier now, November's remote
sun's rays colder,
fog rolls in, covering blue
bay waters, sand beach, brilliant
bare light of summer days we used to head for,
downhill—rhythmic concord that's summoned
awake in walking, and the words that issue
in walking near water and that we pass through
more like windows than doorways
since we look in from so high
off our feet . . .

First light, then faces
brightening the light, sprawled park, sparkling
sea in which I sometimes sense
an almighty god, pitiless at particulars
and argument, asking, "Meaning?
You want meaning? My meaning
equals your gratitude!" and getting
away with it . . .

Eye moving forward, memory back
even to the anguished note fifty years in the voice,
a policeman leading you from a crowd to safety, pleading,
"Please, don't start trouble." How moved you were
by his concern for you, deeper, clearer
than words spoken only a moment ago, fallen into the flood of the instant, making
itself felt only when toppling
forward in the froth . . .

Luckily, nearer, the ditch
calling for attention, rich earth winking blue
iris points as we walked the shore, circling
talk round and in
the same circle of the horizon, resonant
sound's kingdom, sound
of the words we need to spring
to our lips a new breathing in, a new singing out,
words that cannot live alone
any more than we can, hearing our own
voice through our throats, the voice of
others through our ears, saying
there is somewhere we want to go
where no sand blows over the spark of eyes
past the outer channel's curling lipped outrider, beyond
the far islands' depths now milling
your ashes, voice gone

where neither ear nor throat can hear
or hold
from scattering part of what we have
perhaps desperately come to
call immortal, meaning,
that is, unreturnable.

For George Oppen

THE MONTHS OF LOVE

Lying opposite the sun-
capped church dome gleaming
polished mercury across from

sloping Dolores, amid drifting summer
smells—mown grass, split melon, half
sweet baby's breath, half

briny ocean—

you ask their name,
and she calls the bunched white flowering
sprays on the hedgerow above where you lie

"bridal wreath" as you breathe them in,
and the years laid aside in the long
effort at naming rest easy . . .

as though the words open
in the air an invisible window that gives
shape and savor to the light coming through,

letting in the half-acrid, half-alluring
scent fluttering promise you used to head for
in the dry or wet street rainbowed

with gasoline you'd get a stinging whiff of,
the streaked gold- and blue-
scaled benzine snake rippling

beneath car exhaust, then stop and stare
in aching prepubescent wonder, beguiled by
an airborne, promiscuous desire beginning

to call you out of anonymity's
sterile safety, while blurred
heat lulled asleep all sense but

marvel
            wakening
                                    Now as then

sour rot so curiously
mixed with sweet spun
in a breeze from so far back you knew it surely

would outstrip you . . .

And that which has had so much time
in which to be blown away without
a trace is now

more

than ever
here . . . And there
on the outskirts,

in the Panhandle jungle, off the Great Highway beach—
windblown, isolate, snagged hidden
behind bushes, sprouting amid the stench

and mechanical gurgling sea roar
of the cypress-screened sewage plant—
where the hovering homosexuals

glide shyly out, smiling
their tentative, twisted smiles;
let them seduce one another

behind rocks, tall weeds, on the oil-slick sand,
only let them not be left
untouched, faces in a mist held

skewed in the hands of a force demanding
assent, or else leaving
each to stand alone drawing down

despair like a volley ricocheting
from a sniper's gun . . .
and in spite of the odds against them,

nowhere too foul—even here!

O stink-awakened season lately begun,
how many can such as we
name of all the things that can stop

us cold? calling
down like a blow to the eyes too late
what we failed to realize—

breasts to see, to hold in the hand, froth
held between lip and tooth, thighs
to caress, and how much courage it must take

those frightened men to step forth,
this woman who does not believe
she is beautiful, to offer

her loveliness in a sheer cotton dress . . .
And what good if not to free
desire mounting the bone-

dry ladder of the rib cage,
giving, getting, humming-
bird-tongued

head between parted
thighs tasting O good

God!
eye, tongue, nipple
alive
to what
        ever eludes closure

STILL

For Becky Shemis

I hadn't seen my first ocean yet
I used to love to swim

in her tall backyard grass too high to see
anything but blue

and spreading green mold
that happened in summer to life left

standing still. I remember one afternoon
falling over a stone

onto pieces of a milkbottle which hadn't been
there before; I remember getting up, seeing red

blossom where my wrist had divided
blood and space running

to her permanently startled
voice grown husky as her men

kept disappearing from her quick
eyes widening with disbelief,

strong slender hands not moving
to touch rough or smooth again.

Those were days I knew
would pass but did not know

were passing all at once,
though something no more belongs

to then than now and keeps
her from vanishing

and belongs to space,
where all days are one

day as she shows me
herself and my mother, posed rosy

sisters from Aleppo,
before a 1930's shadow-screen

in sepia tones so warm with breath
I am the photographer

of the picture she draws out
from an album she can no longer see,

the words hardly wings, more
like whips to clear the air

for listening to her sore-throated laughing
alarm that nothing in all the days receding

had prepared her for a last look at the sun hardly
brighter than its shadow,

her body making no
sense anymore as she tries to think

of something she will not be able to in time
going out of her arms

into whose hands continually
handing her dishes and everything

tasting the same, O
let me go, you said,

who belong to the hum
there is no word from

FAWAZ TURKI

(1940–)

Fawaz Turki

Born in Haifa, Palestine, in 1940, Fawaz Turki wrote a memoir, *The Disinherited: Journal of a Palestinian Exile* (Monthly Review Press, 1972), which was one of the first, and certainly one of the most acclaimed, books published in America by a Palestinian. Much of the impassioned work concerns Turki's youth living in the refugee camp of Bourj al-Barajneh outside Beirut, and his travels and studies in England, the Orient, and Australia. Written in an intense, short period in Paris, the book is still in print.

Turki has published two poetry books in English; the most recent is *Tel Zaatar Was the Hill of Thyme* (1978), the title poem of which is excerpted here. His long-awaited sequel to *The Disinherited* was published in 1988: *Soul in Exile: Lives of a Palestinian Revolutionary* (Monthly Review Press). A study of Yasser Arafat was also due out in 1988.

Turki has published essays on the fate of the Palestinians in such publications as the *International Herald Tribune*, the *New York Times*, *Worldview*, and the *Journal of Palestine Studies*.

A writer-in-residence at the Virginia Center for the Creative Arts in 1975, Turki was a visiting professor in 1978 at the State University of New York at Buffalo. He has participated in numerous international writers' conferences, including "The Writer and Human Rights," where he served on a panel with Jacobo Timmerman. He was also head of the Palestinian delegation at a 1982 UNESCO conference in Mexico City.

Turki lives in Washington, D.C., and lectures widely.

"The Poet: Response and Responsibility"

Like most Palestinian poets, I draw on my own tragic background for my material. Traditionally in Palestinian society, it is the poet, rather than the ideologue or the theoretician, whose work is taken by the people as a starting point for their pragmatic and metaphoric conjectures on meaning. Hence the role of the poet is both response and responsibility. He internalizes his society's malaise—at this time, its national struggle—and projects it outwardly to the people in his work.

Thus the loftiest place a person in Palestinian culture could aspire to is that occupied by the poet. It is lofty because he is in the vanguard of imposing a coherence on the communal sense of reference for his people. The poet's work must not only reflect his society's aspirations, but attempt to be its window on a life, and aspire to lend dignity to its shattered landscape. He thus denies violence, despair, and death a monopoly of its soul.

IN SEARCH OF YACOVE EVED

Yacove Eved was an Israeli.
In the summer
Yacove Eved always sat on the rocks
in the park at Mount Carmel.
Yacove Eved loved the harbor
and the boats
and the colors as the sun
set in the horizon.
Whenever I saw Yacove Eved on the rocks,
whenever I passed him in the park,
I always said
Salaams Yacove
and Yacove Eved
always waved both his arms
and said *Shalom shaaer*.
Yacove Eved is like me,

he knows all the stabbed dreams
all the ones who died
and who now keep company
with their gods.
So Yacove Eved and I
we sit and talk about this
and we watch the harbor.
Sometimes Yacove Eved
sees me at the port
fishing for the sunken images,
and Yacove Eved says *Salaam shaaer*
and I say *Shalom* Yacove.
Yacove is like me
he knows all the lonely travellers
all the ones who never returned
whose ships are lost at sea.
Now I do not know where
Yacove Eved is
and I do not know where to find him.
I have never known anyone
by that name
but these verses are for him.

MOMENTS OF RIDICULE AND LOVE

In moments of desperation
Palestinian poets wish
they had a government to assail,
politicians,
bureaucrats,
elected bodies
to ridicule.
We never realized
that dragging such comic trivia
into a poem
could be,
like first love,
an exquisite thought.

BEING A GOOD *AMERICANI*

Last Sunday was a fine day
for me to be a good *Americani*.
I painted the kitchen table
and talked to my next door neighbor
while he washed his car.
In between all of that,
I scolded my son for playing
with his genitals,
ate french fries,
fought with my wife
and talked to her mother long distance.
Before it got dark
I hopped in the car
and bought sliced salami,
toilet paper
and a six pack of beer
at 7-Eleven.
At the store
I conversed with the customers
about who shot JR.
The clerk joined in the conversation
and offered a learned
conjecture on who the murderer was.
Soon the sun had set
on Arlington, Virginia,
where I have lived with
my American family for a decade,
trying,
desperately,
to be a good *Americani*.
I watched TV for three hours
and then went to bed.
I thought about our dog
who had died recently.
I would have taken him for a walk

around this time.
My wife hoped I did not mind
that she was not in the mood tonight.
I said honey I don't mind either.
So she combed her blond hair
and I read *Time* magazine.
I had my life
figured out cold for me.
Only from time to time
I wake up in the middle of the night,
or maybe somewhere when the night
is just fading into day,
when the moment
is neither here nor there,
which is a safe time to think
about Palestine and olive trees,
and I pity myself
and the place I came from.

From TEL ZAATAR WAS THE HILL OF THYME

I leave the child to grow up by itself as a beggar from the killing zone. In Lebanon where the spider web from colonial past had glued its sticky fingers to the land. Heaven is full of children who died in September. Every winter they fall to the ground.

In the United States, I say I am twenty five hundred years old. That is why I speak English with a mocking voice. Americans have endured the ultimate in pain. When I ask them why, they say our homes have gone to superhighways and *McHale's Navy* is no longer being shown, even in reruns.

It is like thin ice here. In this country. If you dig deep with your feet or roots or mind or vision, you sink like a stone. Except for the salt smells drifting from the ghettos. Where black children fall on their heads reaching after the one remaining rotten apple on the tree.

I wander around America throwing off thick heat.

Hey, don't do that, do you hear? Don't throw off thick heat around here. Don't make waves. When I knew J.O. at home, he had wanted to be Hannibal scaling the mountains, smashing the obstacles in his way, including the communities of flowers, to Return. In the United States, and for twelve years, he listened to Walter every night and did not throw off thick heat, till his own question about himself no longer startled anyone. Palestine was still rhythm and vision was still song, but neither was music. I am too abused by time. Listen. I am too abused by time.

The time of Tel Zaatar.

Tel Zaatar was the Hill of Thyme. Tel Zaatar was crazed by thirst. Yet water lived on the edge of a world, on the edge of continents on the edge of cities on the edge of hills. Except the Hill of Thyme, home to 30,000 Palestinians; and for close to three score years, home to the white morning light. And some crazy shadows. Home to a people living there in a kind of silent orgy of intricate sounds. The Hill stood off the city, reclining detachedly from it, as if to make the statement that it is in the Arab world, but not of it. And the years sped, one after the other, to hug one another, body and soul. What stood between the Hill and the world, all this time, was the Hill's knife and the world's silence. The Hill's weapon, though, was a mere shrivelled up memory of an aggregate of Palestinian childhoods. And these were silhouetted against the walls of the mudhouses, proclaiming a formality of their own. A separateness of tone. A kind of absurd purity.

It was not just the water that dried up when the siege of the Hill started. For even before that, children died in simple silence. The ones who did not die in silence, died after the fall of the Hill. The ones that survived the fall, died in the long trek to the Western side of the city. And the ones that remained alive, through it all, who had felt the cruel finger of more than fifteen winters and then seen the forty-three varieties of ritual terror in the forty-three days of siege—these few will now lie in wait for the coming of every bitter spring, with their hands reaching out for tough argument. And someone will then smother their screams and their fury. Someone will. For the children of the Hill are like that. I am from their hill and of their pain. For I grew up on a neighboring hill that we called Borj el Barajena, or the Tower of Towers; and when I recall it, in a flash of images, I get only a pungence of nameless pain.

I want to talk about Tel Zaatar because I like my voice and I like my pain. I like them in my aloneness, because only in it can I define our Palestinian solitude in a fraternity of screams of sunrise.

I have a blank page with me. And the dumb keys of a typewriter. With these I am supposed to paint a portrait of the geography of the soul of a whole community of men, women and children who had survived the siege and fall of their Hill. It is so helpless a project. So vain. And so absurd. It is like my Palestinian childhood in the muddy lane of the Tower of Towers and the ghettos of Beirut, when I would stomp my feet, lusting after the taste of unspecific afternoons, stretching back, backwards, to Palestine. Between then and now, between the Tower of Towers and the Hill of Thyme, between my original leap to a maturing consciousness and my helpless rage, lies my Palestinian sensibility. Thus when I roamed foreign cities, all these years, I never window shopped for ideologies. I already had one. I just looked for stores that sold guillotines. For soon—sure it must be soon—the case of those who set siege to the Hill will come up for trial.

They called themselves fascists, they who besieged the Hill. Their ideology was the ultimate code of the bully. Their vision a denial of human compassion.

It is the duty of every Lebanese to kill one Palestinian.

Fascists surround the Hill from every direction. They pound it with artillery shells, day and night. Day and night. Day and night. There is no respite between the setting of the sun and the break of dawn, between the noon sun and the afternoon wind. The big bow flies, along with the emaciated dogs and cats, feed on the dead bodies that lie in the lanes, the front yards of abandoned homes and around the water pumps. The first child dies from a dog bite, and an order is given by the commanders of the Resistance to kill all dogs and cats. Fear of death from rabies is added to the fear of death from dehydration, thirst, starvation, unattended wounds and from living in a place with such a lyric name.

Fascist snipers are perched around the Hill to shoot at anyone and anything that moves. Fascist guns pound any structure that is not already in ruins. The Hill of Thyme became the testing ground for the world's modern weaponry. Syrian weapons from the Soviet Union, Lebanese weapons from France, fascist weapons from Israel.

Among the forty-three days of siege someone who was not there sobbed with pain. But what is the use of empathetic pain, especially when experienced on Connecticut Avenue? It is just that you know a fragment, another fragment, of inky black darkness is added to your history. But its enormity belongs to me, and that is why, from the time a gaudy twilight closed its fist on the Hill of Thyme, the story of Tel Zaatar will etch itself on my skin.

On another day during the siege—was it at the start or the end of it, at the beginning or the end of our eternity—I spoke on the phone to someone "over there" in Beirut.

How is it, Um Adnan?

She shrieked the quintessence of sixty years of grief into the receiver.

May the Lord pour acid on their souls and their homes and their honor. May the Lord destroy the house they built.

We come from the womb of a mother, they believe, who is an outlaw, an outcast against whom the world should protect their nations. Palestine should now hide from the sun. There is no place under it for our own nation. And Tel Zaatar laughs at the philistines and their absurd notions.

Around the Hill, the fascists tell each other and the world that they believed in the Father, the Son and the Holy Ghost. They have pictures of the Virgin Mary taped on their guns and helmets. Inside the Hill of Thyme, the screams of human suffering lash out like the tail of a rabid history. Napalm canisters roll on the roofs, side by side, end over end, and burn the hill. And blood leaps on the walls. In the sky, jets pierce a long trail. The ideology of this Arab world, around the Hill of Thyme, rattles its sounds like the dirt under the fingernails of all the dead bodies in our mass graves. There is a strong desire, a formidable desire, to see death inflicted on Palestinians in this part of the world. There is a season, every now and again, when Palestinians should die, like the prairie grass to be burnt for the new season of crops.

In Bloody April of 1948, we sobbed in rooms that had no windows. In Helpless June of 1967, we ran helter skelter across the Allenby Bridge and our children, in the panic, found no hands to hold. In Black September of 1970, there was no time to bury all the dead because motorcycle gangs wanted our hills for their turf. And in between then and the siege of our Hill of Thyme, jets with air-conditioned cockpits dropped their loads of incendiary bombs on us.

I am not tired of watching a heroic scene. I am just tired of books that describe it. I am tired of my own books, of fleeing into the confines of my poems where I am sure of shelter.

I know, one day, I will meet one of the children whose bodies were set on fire, who died of dehydration, defending the Hill of Thyme. I will meet one of them, and I will tear off my skin with grief and ram my head against his eternity. Above all, I will cut my fingers off. For what is the use of hitting them on the keys of a typewriter, in my study, in my comfortable diaspora dream, in order to write a poem and play with my child on a carpeted floor, and complain to myself that the whole world is taking its revenge on the defenseless children of our exiled nation?

Yet always I feel the exquisiteness of infinite numbers walking side by side, arm in arm, with our history. On the Hill of Thyme. In the Tower of Towers. With Izz el Deen el Kassam. After Karameh. Inside Palestine. During the Return.

DORIS SAFIE

(1940–)

Doris Safie

Doris Safie came to the United States via El Salvador, to which both sets of grandparents had emigrated from Palestine in the early years of the century. When she was six months old many members of her family moved north, eventually settling in Brooklyn and, later, in Rye, New York. She was educated in the public schools and at Marymount Secondary School in Tarrytown, then made New York City her home; in 1969, she received her B.A. in oriental studies and linguistics from Columbia University. She moved to Vermont in 1981 and received her M.F.A. in creative writing from Vermont College in 1984. Her poems have since appeared in *Cedar Rock* and *Calliope*. Safie is also an aspiring playwright and has been engaged with the Vermont Repertory Theatre of Burlington. Safie works at the telephone company in New London, New Hampshire, where she currently lives.

"Bones"

I want to tell you about bones. Safie bones. Zabaneh bones. Canafati and Salman bones. Uburzi-Zamora-Gravi-Hishme-Barake-Wakile-Zacarias-Khalil-Handal-Said-Kattan-Hasbun-and-heaven-knows-what-else bones. Direct connectors and lateral ones. The kind that make you move, that hold you up.

I never thought about bones, until I broke one. But I forgot about it until many years had passed, and a few of my bones started telling me secrets. One was about an ancestor who tore off her veil and cut it into strips which she shaped into elegant Arabic letters. Another was about an ancestor who was playing by the sea when he found a bottle with a message in it that said he would find treasure if he married a girl who tore off her veil. He bumped into her one day, and they produced many treasures.

Several centuries later, a 16-year-old girl cousin of these two wrote a poem about a virgin called Mary who lived in "an unknown land." A group called the "Court Cherubim, #108, Catholic Daughters of America of the Tarrytowns" liked the poem enough to give her a prize. What the girl didn't know then was that her bones were beginning to tell her something. But she remained suspended between the "unknown land" of her ancestors, and the "unknown land" where people said things like "Oh gee, you one o' them A-rabs?" Suspended in a pudding of submission—the traditional Catholic sort, the one that meant "Islam" in Arabic, and the kind that was expected of her as a girl.

Approaching middle age, her bones became voluble. They told her that poetry was a land that could be known only by submitting to its imperatives. It had something to do with tearing off veils, with heeding messages hidden in bottles. It hung on a frame of bone-words. And it insisted that a poet have no nation, but that he carry his nation within him.

So it came to pass that the girl became a woman who discovered that earning her life was more important than earning a living. And she felt very lucky. Because even though she was living in a country too young to have poetry embedded in its marrow, she had become imbued with its questing spirit, and she had use of its beautiful

English tongue with which to tell of the secrets within her. And even though she had become isolated from her roots and lacked the use of the beautiful Arabic tongue, she carried in her bones the proclivity towards poetry that the desert had honed to an instinct in her ancestors.
Who needs roots when you have bones? The kind that talk to you as you earn your death.

DANGER, MEN IN TREES

Quietly, they take on the color and shape
of their surroundings. The danger lies
in the knowing. He said he had to find
the animal in himself. I said I already knew
where it was. But he went anyway,

when the branches were bare and full
of regret, as if time had a shape
that hangs from a straw. By the time
the leaves came, as they must
when rain and sun collude in spring,
I couldn't even see him. I looked

for the other women, and we talked,
over tea. We talked and talked until

the children came running in and shouted,
We can see them through the fox rain!
Sure enough, we could make out their limbs—
poised on the edge of raindrops
slanting gently down the sun's beams—
on the verge of gliding past the horizon.

That night, the wolf moon's yellow grin
slid past my window, daring me to spy
into its clouded face. And I remembered
the first time I saw him, across the street,
holding an open umbrella, when it seemed his lips
were as close to mine as mine were to my mouth.

What excited me was their unknown quantity,
the feeling that makes you cling to straws.

I grew bored looking through windows, went out
to the indelible night, urged by the memory
of the thud inside me when he'd casually toss
a newspaper on the sofa. Or the rattle
cups made in their saucers, each time his arm
brushed the air in reaching for salt.

I looked back at the house, and the lights
grew dim, but I knew the power company
would have no record of it. I looked back
at the sky, and knew if I watched him
I'd change his course forever.

MEDITATION BY THE XEROX MACHINE

For Ethel Weinberger

Such a gloomy day
rain rain rain
sound of soldiers
in rain this gray
because of the rain
to believe something
in this small town trapped
by rain, mountains frame
the window, my hand
on the glass, coming out gray
on gray two three four
promising black and white
two three such ennui

in terms of global warfare is
vicious, has an edge, a child

of cities paved with children whose
bones echo, empty
drums. I copy and copy
and copy, dead paper
flies out like dry tongues, craving

the art of a poem you want
about peace. And I'd give you
the sun and its light dreaming
of seeds that burst
so flowers might bloom, a leak
of imagination and love to break
dams, melt ice, soften this earth too
subtle with hope, but this rain
these dead children gnaw at me gray
with numbness. I watch
two drops merge, like your dream
of a horse with wings connecting
continents at war. It's a choice
of no choice, this art in me
that wails, claws at the soul
like rain scratching
the window. The man in me
envies conviction, the woman
fears it, the child waits, the child
who says it likes rats
and moles, especially dead
ones. I know it's just a phase but
these crucifixions cling
like burrs. I keep trying
and trying and trying to find
the jewel in the machine in this room

that tolls the music of dead
masters, lost in the whirr of the machine
that blurs the tender craft of those
who see, as I copy and copy and copy . . .

IN THE MIDDLE OF READING ONE MORE POEM WITH BRUEGHEL AS A METAPHOR

I'm sick of poems with Brueghel
in them, and bats, bones . . .
I had an aunt
once, she had a sweet shop.
She sold dried
plums in a beige country
below the equator.
Her eyes were like the plums
round and hard. She
could see everything.
Whenever she saw me
(I was little then)
she kissed me twice—
once on each cheek, hard
snaps that sucked
my dimples and left
impressions.
She always
smelled of sugar. Not
the flour stuff you
get here. I mean
the raw stuff
like gravel. That
was her voice, too, sweet
pebbles that smoothed,
left you gasping.
She didn't know from Brueghel.
As for bats
they don't grow in beige
countries.
Her bones? Well,
she carried them around
like everyone else.
And when she tired

of them, the earth
was happy
to have them. Which is why
poems with Brueghel in them
and bats etcetera
leave me cold.

BEN BENNANI

(1946–)

Ben Bennani

Ben Bennani was born in Seer, a summer resort town north of Tripoli, Lebanon, and was educated in classical Arabic literature in Tripoli. He is a graduate of Dartmouth College and holds an M.F.A. in poetry and a Ph.D. in comparative literature, as well as a graduate certificate in translation theory and practice. He has taught writing, translation, and literature at the University of Massachusetts, University of Wyoming, State University of New York (Binghamton), Northeastern University, and Georgia Southwestern College. He continues to edit and publish *Paintbrush: A Journal of Poetry, Translations, and Letters*, which he founded in 1974.

His poems and translations have appeared in over fifty literary magazines in the United States, England, and Canada, while his works of translation include *Splinters of Bone: Poems by Mahmud Darwish* (Greenfield Review Press, 1974), and *Bread, Hashish, and Moon: Four Modern Arab Poets* (Unicorn Press, 1982). Collections of his own poetry include *A Bowl of Sorrow* (Greenfield Review Press, 1977) and *Camel's Bite* (Jelm Mountain Press, 1980). Currently, he teaches English and creative writing at Northeast Missouri State University.

"This Vast Self"

Poetry is knowledge which cannot be expressed in prose. It requires an orchestration of sound, music, image, and connotation of word to express. In that way, poetry overcomes the limits of both language and music.

Poets everywhere have often carried an aura of madness. Plato banished them from his utopian society. I honor the holes in their sandals' soles, for "the vast expanse / Of the poet's self enhances / The certainty of madness / That seldom dwells in his house / Of hair." I feel that this vast self is present in everyone but is accessible to only a few who have the ability to feel and see it—those who are driven *to tell what they know.*

That is why I wanted to become a poet. It was both the ability and the need to answer questions in more than one dimension. It began with words, with seeing *in words what words really are. In* "Le mot juste" *I profess that "Word is / just / a spirit / an ape / hairy here / & there / nude / has a mind / of its own / prism / prickly / but mute & consequently / rude."*

The "Arabness" of my poetic self gives me the heritage of a culture in which poetry is the record of the mind, the soul, and the spirit of a people. In America, unfortunately, poetry most often presents the individual in isolation; that, too, is reflected in my poetry. Serious poetry itself occupies a small place in the pop, bang, fast-road culture of America which I decry in "Seeing America from Behind":

> *Now that the porch has skipped town*
> *and the lawn rolled down Memory Lane*
> *The backyard, fenced and fancy,*
> *Has become America's playground.*
> *Unlike children, neighbors are heard*
> *Not seen, often sniffed at as well*
> *Like animals sniff strangers*
> *Through the bars of their cages.*

LETTERS TO LEBANON

For My Mother

Good morning, sad priestess,
and a kiss for your wet cheek.
It's me! Sinbad,
your senseless son
who moons ago
took off on his fantastic voyage.
Don't you remember how he packed
the green morning of home
inside his faded bag,
stuffing his clean underwear
with little bundles
of dried mint leaves?

I'm alone now.
The smoke bores the cigarette.
The typewriter is bored.
My pains are clowns
searching for a circus tent.
Yes, I've known women in America
—cement sentiments
and beauty carved of wood.

Say hello to my room,
to my bed and books,
to the children
on our block,
to walls we decorated
with chaotic writing,
to lazy cats sleeping on windowsills
covered with lilacs.

It's been years, Mother,
since I left Tangier,

its saffron suns
and listless seas, or Seer
and its walnut trees.
November is here;
he brings his presents pressingly:
tears and moans at my windowpane
and November is here.
Where is Tangier?
Where is Lebanon?
I hear the U.S. Marines
are looking for her
among the mines and mice
in the fields.
Tell them, Mother,
lest more get hurt,
she's right here
—gored and bleeding
like her beloved Adonis.
I've dressed her wounds
with eucalyptus leaves
from the East
and bandaged them
with gauze of Western snow.
I've swaddled her
in Father's old prayer rug.

Where is Father?
Where are his eyes
and the silk of their look?
Don't forget his Turkish coffee!
Is he still adamant
about the cardamon?
Where is the open yard
of our large house?
Carnations chuckled
in the shade of its corners.
Where is my childhood?
I dragged cats by their tails
across the open yard.

I'm alone now.
My pains are birds
searching for a nest.

CAMEL'S BITE

The sour grapes I saw in Aleppo
Turned up as raisins in Morocco;
I learned that the vast expanse
Of the poet's self enhances
The certainty of madness
That seldom dwells in his house
Of hair. It's lethal and finite
Like a camel's occasional bite.
Like an ancient Arab poet
Half oracle, half ogre, I anoint
My hair on one side of my head,
Let my mantle hang down loosely
And wear only one sandal. I start
An oasis in the sun's deep belly.

SHARIF S. ELMUSA

(1947–)

Sharif S. Elmusa

Sharif S. Elmusa was born in the village of Abbasiyah outside Jaffa, Palestine, in 1947. His father grew figs, grapes, and the famous Jaffa orange in his groves. Within a year of his birth, the family was made refugees. In the Jordan Valley, Elmusa's father switched from farming fruit to farming vegetables and with his wife raised twelve children at the refugee camp of Nuweimeh in Jericho.

Elmusa, the fifth child, went to high school in Jericho and Jerusalem and then attended Cairo University in Egypt. In 1971, he came to Boston, graduated with a Master's Degree in Civil Engineering from Northeastern University, and worked until 1977 as a civil engineer. In 1987, he received his Ph.D. from the Urban Studies and Planning Department at the Massachusetts Institute of Technology. He has published two books: *A Harvest of Technology: The Super-green Revolution in the Jordan Valley* (Center for Contemporary Arab Studies, Georgetown University, 1994) and *Water Conflict: Economics, Politics, Law, and the Palestinian-Israeli Water Resources* (Institute for Palestine Studies, 1997).

Elmusa's poetry has appeared in *Poetry East*, *Greenfield Review*, and the *Christian Science Monitor* and was nominated for the Pushcart Prize in 1984. His translations of Arabic poetry appear in *Modern Arabic Poetry* (Columbia University Press, 1987) and *On Entering the Sea: The Erotic and Other Poetry of Nizar Qabbani* (Interlink Publishing, 1996).

At present Elmusa is an associate professor of political science at the American University in Cairo. He lives with his wife and children in Washington, D.C.

"Poetry as Cocoon"

In school I loved both poetry and math. (Later I read that someone had defined the poetic image as a theorem without a proof.) The result was first a restless detour through science and engineering, then a more reconciled coexistence with political economy of development. But poetry chooses us, as Yevtushenko said. And when it welled again, I felt as if a missing leg was restored. Yet in today's single-specialty world, one sometimes feels, or is made to feel, a trespasser.

It need not be so; it was not always so. To the Arab "thinkers" of Andalusia, at the zenith of its fluorescence in art and science, we are told

> *. . . it would have seemed meaningless to ask if science were not in some danger of making men hard, calculating, overintellectual, cold, insensitive to beauty and art. Their students of science were commonly poets and musicians. That there was any antagonism between the intellectual and emotional life, that both could not be cultivated by the same person, would have seemed to them a paradox (Joseph McCabe, quoted in Idries Shah,* The Sufis*).*

Such a stance was rooted in the belief that identification and detachment were indispensable training for the self. Too much identification with one thing, be it person, doctrine, country, or even discipline, is bound to lead to fanaticism and, when the object of our attachment fails us, despair. A society enamored of logic and efficiency breeds Dr. Strangeloves. As Walt Whitman listened to the "learned astronomer" hammer out figures and chart pathways of the stars giving no inkling that he was moved by their beauty, the poet grew sick and tired, rushed out of the lecture hall, and stared in perfect silence at the sky. Perhaps if the Pentagon chiefs took time to write poems, they might decide that the stars, not to speak of the cherry blossoms next to them, were too beautiful to be mined with infernal missiles.

On the opposite pole, the division of life into fields, ever shrinking into smaller parcels of expertise, leaves poets only the fields of their own selves and poetry to explore. Poets, by and large, seem to resign themselves to their own ration and, like other specialists, permeate their work with differential equations and talk to themselves and a handful of literati. Releasing poetry from its cocoon, if anybody cares to, is a challenge to society, as well as poets.

SHE FANS THE WORD

(*For my daughter*)

A word
round and full
finally blooms
on the raw tongue
of the child.
It makes her giddy.
She fans the word
by her bear
and bunny
by the flowers
in the vase
by the strange forms
in the mirror
by the water
breaking loose
from the hose.
She fans the word
as a peacock fans
its tail
as a man his windfall,
unsure of having,
afraid of losing it.

THE TWO ANGELS

Among the things mother told me
as a child:

Every person has two angels
standing on his shoulders;
they weigh every deed.
On the right *Nakir*,
for the good deeds;
for the bad, *Nakeer*, on the left.

That is why my gait is tilted now
and as the years pass
my back will grow hunched.

Such nakedness!

BOOKISHNESS

I once had a lover
bewitched by novels.
She was always reading, reading
and reticent;
and she was right,
"One cannot tell whole stories."
Naturally,
I stopped asking
and pretended reading—anything.
A Guide To Birds, Ask Beth, A Vision of Hell,
even poetry.
In bed she'd lie, naked,
except for the glasses.
I took them off.
Her eyes were deep blue,
deeper than you think,

hypnotic. Her hair
was distinguished
although not yet grey.
    She also read my body
precisely,
till one night,
holding me close, she cried,
"Yes, yes, handsome Ieyasu."

SNAPSHOTS

"Amman is softer / than the skin of goats."
—A bedouin poet

In the blink of an eye
flesh and cement
take over its ancient hills.

No river wets its throat.
The wisps of grass
turn yellow
under the first footfalls
of summer,

and the few birds
that come by
look puzzled, pained
like migrant workers.

*

Up and down the steep hills,
cars, humped like camels,
issue their pleas.

In the minaret
God gets used
to loudspeakers.

IN THE REFUGEE CAMP

The huts were of mud and hay,
their thin roofs feared the rain,
and walls slouched like humbled men.
The streets were laid out in a grid,
as in New York,
but without the dignity of names
or asphalt. Dust reigned.
Women grew pale
chickens and children
feeding them fables from the lost land.
And a madman sawed the minaret
where a melodious voice
cried for help on behalf of the believers.

Of course I gazed at the sky
on clear nights,
at stars drizzling
soft grains of light,
at the moon's deliberate face,
at the good angel wrapped in purple air.
  I had no ladder
and nothing from heaven fell
in my crescent hands.

Ah, how I cursed Adam and Eve
and the ones who made them refugees.

FATHER LULLABIES THE UNBORN

Locust,
see how the seed I cast
nips the pulp and leaves
of my lover

Rain,
see how the seed I cast
rises in the stem of my lover
how it kneads her breast
a wild white flower

Lord,
see how the seed I cast
flutters my hand like a prayer
like a star around its firmament

Song,
see how the seed I cast
stirs the roots of my tongue:
Albi ala waladi
wa alb waladi alhajar—
my heart enfolds my child
and my child enfolds the stone

Fisherman,
see how the seed I cast
breaks my bottle
and summons me from my smoke,
a frightened genie.

EXPATRIATES

The moon, neither full nor crescent, leans
35° toward the plane of melancholy. Jupiter
is missing, in its place a space for pondering.
Two anonymous stars leap from the constellation,
hand in hand. Blackberries fill the dipper.

A meteor falls, mad,
in the blaze Van Gogh, Attila József,
martyred for the nation of poetry.
Whereas Neruda pushes the walls of his trench
underground, still refusing to die.

I intend to live my ration of years and hours,
no more, no less. And when my boots grow heavy
I will think how that caterpillar
wove her cocoon on the sand of the beach,
how a nun might giggle riding a Ferris wheel.

DREAM ON THE SAME MATTRESS

Welcome
to the tribe of the wed.
But before you enter
the tent
let me stitch a patch or two
onto your quilt.

Resilience,
a shrewd caliph once said,
is the golden rule
of politics.
Resilience, my kinsfolk,
is the diamond rule
of marriage.
This cord of love
that binds you now
keep it taut—
give when she pulls
and pull when he gives.

Marriage is a rose garden
where squash is fond to grow.
Accept them both:
The spirit seeks
inspiration
and the stomach
sustenance.

Do not eat from the same dish,
said Gibran;
            but the prophet never married.
Drink from the same cup,
                        I say,
and dream on the same mattress.

LAWRENCE JOSEPH

(1948–)

Lawrence Joseph

Lawrence Joseph was born in Detroit in 1948. His grandparents were Lebanese and Syrian Catholic immigrants. He was educated at the University of Michigan, where he received first prize in the Hopwood Poetry Award; Cambridge University, where he read English; and the University of Michigan Law School. His first book of poems, *Shouting at No one*, received the 1982 Agnes Lynch Starret Poetry Prize from the University of Pittsburgh Press. His second book, *Curriculum Vitae*, was published by the University of Pittsburgh Press in 1988.

Joseph, an attorney, clerked for the Michigan Supreme Court before he became an associate professor of law at the University of Detroit School of Law. He then practiced law in New York City. He presently is a professor of law at St. John's University School of Law.

In 1984 Joseph received a National Endowment for the Arts Poetry Award. He is married to the painter Nancy Van Goethem and lives in New York City.

"Making Myself Understood"

It is 1951; I am three years old. My mother and father worry about me because when I try and talk I have great difficulty making myself understood.

It is a late winter or early spring late afternoon in the living room of my grandparents' house in Pleasant Ridge, Michigan, a small suburb two miles north of Detroit. My parents, my brother, and I live with my father's mother and father. Father, mother, brother, grandmother, grandfather define me; the Lebanon from which my grandparents emigrated thirty-five years before and the Detroit to which they came defines us.

That afternoon the curtains are half drawn. Light brown, golden light cuts the room into shadows. I touch the latticed glass door between the living room and the sunroom, fascinated by the spectrum of colors the glass absorbs and reflects and, suddenly, the door opens. In the sunroom, in the same shadows and light, grandpa sits alone. He does not see me see him. What I see are his eyes—his soft, tired, permanently sad, alive eyes. I don't know what he sees.

All of my poetry is, perhaps, the attempt to explain this oldest memory of mine, a witnessed time and witnessed place which existed neither in time nor place—that mysterious blessing from my Lebanese grandpa.

Soon grandpa was dead, his gangrened legs amputated, his arteries filled with too much life and death. Soon after his death, when I talked I made myself understood.

CURRICULUM VITAE

I might have been born in Beirut,
not Detroit, with my right name.
Grandpa taught me to love to eat.
I am not Orthodox, or Sunni,
Shiite, or Druse. Baptized
in the one true Church, I too
was weaned on Saint Augustine.

Eisenhower never dreamed I wore
corrective shoes. Ford Motor Co.
never cared I'd never forgive
Highland Park, River Rouge, Hamtramck.
I memorized the Baltimore Catechism.
I collected holy cards, prayed
to a litany of saints to intercede
on behalf of my father who slept
through the sermon at 7 o'clock Mass.
He worked two jobs, believed
himself a failure. My brother
believed himself, my sister denied.
In the fifth grade Sister Victorine,
astonished, listened to me recite
from the Book of Jeremiah.
My voice changed. I wanted women.
The Jesuit whose yellow fingers
cracked with the stink of Camels
promised me eternal punishment.
How strange I was, with impure thoughts,
brown skin, obsessions.
You could tell by the way I walked
I possessed a lot of soul,
you could tell by the way I talked
I didn't know when to stop.
After I witnessed stabbings
outside the gym, after the game,
I witnessed fire in the streets.
My head set on fire in Cambridge,
England, in the Whim Café.
After I applied Substance and Procedure
and Statements of Facts
my head was heavy as earth.
Now years have passed since
I came to the city of great fame.
The same sun glows gray on two new rivers.
Tears I want do not come.
I remain many different people.
whose families populate half Detroit;

I hate the racket of the machines,
the oven's heat, curse
bossmen behind their backs.
I hear the inmates' collective murmur
in the jail on Beaubien Street.
I hear myself say, "What explains
the Bank of Lebanon's liquidity?"
think, "I too will declare
a doctrine upon whom the loss
of language must fall regardless
whether Wallace Stevens
understood senior indebtedness
in Greenwich Village in 1906."
One woman hears me in my sleep
plead the confusions of my dream.
I frequent the Café Dante, earn
my memories, repay my moods.
I am as good as my heart.
I am as good as the unemployed
who wait in long lines for money.

THEN

Joseph Joseph breathed slower
as if that would stop
the pain splitting his heart.
He turned the ignition key
to start the motor and leave
Joseph's Food Market to those
who wanted what was left.
Take the canned peaches,
take the greens, the turnips,
drink the damn whiskey
spilled on the floor,
he might have said.
Though fire was eating half
Detroit, Joseph could only think
of how his father,

with his bad legs, used to hunch
over the cutting board
alone in light particled
with sawdust behind
the meat counter, and he began
to cry. Had you been there
you would have been thinking
of the old Market's wooden walls
turned to ash or how Joseph's whole arm
had been shaking as he stopped
to pick up an onion,
and you would have been afraid.
You wouldn't have known
that soon Joseph Joseph would stumble,
his body paralyzed an instant
from neck to groin.
You would simply have shaken your head
at the tenement named "Barbara" in flames
or the Guardsman with an M-16
looking in the window of Dave's Playboy Barbershop,
then closed your eyes
and murmured, This can't be.
You wouldn't have known
it would take nine years
before you'd realize the voice howling in you
was born then.

NOT YET

When my father breathed
unevenly I breathed
unevenly, I prayed
in St. Maron's Cathedral
for the strength
of a cedar tree
and for the world to change.
When I saw my father's tears
I did not pray;

I hated our grocery store
where the bullet
barely missed his heart,
I hoped the mists exhaled
by the Vale of Esk
in a country of lakes
4,000 miles away
would be mine.
That was before
Lopez whispered through his rotten teeth
behind a maze of welding guns,
"You're colored, like me,"
before I knew
there is so much
anger in my
heart,
so much need
to avenge the holy cross
and the holy card
with its prayers for the dead,
so many words
I have no choice to say.
Years without enough to make me
stop talking!
I want it all.
I don't want
the angel inside me, sword in hand,
to be silent.
Not yet.

IT'S NOT ME SHOUTING AT NO ONE

Before dawn, on the street again,
beneath the sky that washes me
with ice, smoke, metal
I don't want to think
the bullet pierced my shoulder,
the junkie's rotten teeth

laughed, his yellow hair froze.
I'm careful: I smoke
Turkish tobacco cigarette butts,
I drink a lot to piss a lot,
I fry the pig in its own fat,
eat the knuckles, brain, and stomach;
I don't eat the eyes!
Always four smokestacks
burning bones, somewhere
tears that won't stop,
everywhere blood becomes
flesh that wants to say something.
It's not me shouting at no one
in Cadillac Square: it's God
roaring inside me, afraid
to be alone.

SAND NIGGER

In the house in Detroit
in a room of shadows
when grandma reads her Arabic newspaper
it is difficult for me to follow her
word by word from right to left
and I do not understand
why she smiles about the Jews
who won't do business in Beirut
"because the Lebanese
are more Jew than Jew,"
or whether to believe her
that if I pray
to the holy card of Our Lady of Lebanon
I will share the miracle.
Lebanon is everywhere
in the house: in the kitchen
of steaming pots, leg of lamb
in the oven, plates of kousa,

hushwee rolled in cabbage,
dishes of olives, tomatoes, onions,
roasted chicken and sweets;
at the card table in the sunroom
where grandpa teaches me
to wish the dice across the backgammon board
to the number I want;
Lebanon of mountains and sea,
of pine and almond trees,
of cedars in the service
of Solomon, Lebanon
of Babylonians, Phoenicians, Arabs, Turks
and Byzantines, of the one-eyed
monk, Saint Maron,
in whose rite I am baptized;
Lebanon of my mother
warning my father not to let
the children hear,
of my brother who hears
and from whose silence
I know there is something
I will never know; Lebanon
of grandpa giving me my first coin
secretly, secretly
holding my face in his hands,
kissing me and promising me
the whole world.
My father's vocal cords bleed;
he shouts too much
at his brother, his partner,
in the grocery store that fails.
I hide money in my drawer, I have
the talent to make myself heard.
I am admonished to learn,
never to dirty my hands
with sawdust and meat.
At dinner, a cousin

describes his niece's head
severed with bullets, in Beirut,
in civil war. "More than
an eye for an eye," he demands,
breaks down, and cries.
My uncle tells me to recognize
my duty, to use my mind,
to bargain, to succeed.
He turns the diamond ring
on his finger, asks if
I know what asbestosis is,
"the lungs become like this,"
he says, holding up a fist;
he is proud to practice
law which "distributes
money to compensate flesh."
Outside the house my practice
is not to respond to remarks
about my nose or the color of my skin.
"Sand nigger," I'm called,
and the name fits: I am
the light-skinned nigger
with black eyes and the look
difficult to figure—a look
of indifference, a look to kill—
a Levantine nigger
in the city on the strait
between the great lakes Erie and St. Clair
which has a reputation
for violence, an enthusiastically
bad-tempered sand nigger
who waves his hands, nice enough
to pass, Lebanese enough
to be against his brother,
with his brother against his cousin,
with cousin and brother
against the stranger.

THAT'S ALL

I work and I remember. I conceive
a river of cracked hands above Manhattan.

No spirit leaped with me in the womb.
No prophet explains why Korean women

thread Atomic Machinery's machines
behind massive, empty criminal tombs.

Why do I make my fire my heart's blood,
two or three ideas thought through

to their conclusions, make my air
dirty the rain around towers of iron,

a brown moon, the whole world?
My power becomes my sorrow.

Truth? My lies are sometimes true.
Firsthand, I now see the God

whose witness is revealed in tongues
before the Exchange on Broad Street

and the transfer of 2,675,000,000 dollars
by tender offer are acts of the mind,

and the calculated truths of First
National City Bank. Too often

I think about third cousins in the Shouf.
I also often think about the fact that

in 1926, after Céline visited
the Ford Rouge foundry and wrote

his treatise on the use of physically
inferior production line workers,

an officially categorized "displaced person"
tied a handkerchief around his face

to breathe the smells and the heat
in a manner so as not to destroy

his lungs and brain for four years
until he was laid off. I don't

meditate on hope and despair.
I don't deny the court that rules

my race is Jewish or Abyssinian.
In good times I transform myself

into the sun's great weight, in bad times
I make myself like smoke on flat wastes.

I don't know why I choose who I am:
I work and I remember, that's all.

GREGORY ORFALEA

(1949–)

Gregory Orfalea

Born in downtown Los Angeles in 1949, Gregory Orfalea grew up in a women's garment-making family near orange groves surrounding the city. His grandparents were Syro-Lebanese immigrants; one grandmother continues to water the tallest flowering eucalyptus in Pasadena.

Orfalea's poetry, fiction, and essays have appeared in, among others, *Los Angeles Times Magazine, Triquarterly, Wahington Post,* and the *Antioch Review.* He is the author of *Messengers of the Lost Battalion* (The Free Press/Simon and Schuster, 1997), a memoir of his father and his parachute battalion in World War II, *Before the Flames: A Quest for the History of Arab Americans* (The University of Texas Press, 1988), and two poetry collections, *The Capital of Solitude* and *Pictures at an Exhibition.*

The recipient of the Edward B. Bunn Award for Journalistic Excellence on graduation from Georgetown University, Orfalea took an M.F.A. degree in creative writing from the University of Alaska and has worked as a daily newspaper reporter, editor, and teacher.

Currently an editor with the U.S. Department of Health and Human Services, Orfalea resides with his wife and three sons in Washington, D.C.

"Preserve"

I have always been a writer concerned about our solitude and the need to extend ourselves literarily and literally to combat the almost natural callousness of our times. However, with the sudden death two years ago of my father and sister, the world of politics became insubstantial, papery. The only solid thing in my life was the loss. It was a body I carried and carry now, more compelling than my own.

I should also add, not so much with embarrassment as with dread, it became more compelling than the impulse to write poetry. "Silences," as Tillie Olsen described them, can affect men as well as women, and though they may be caused by a plethora of obligations, they may also come from something like psychic shock.

Since the black day the surviving members of my immediate family began, almost imperceptibly, to come back to life. And it appears each has done so by a kind of self-obliteration. We were ever watchful of each other—the temptation to flee in so many ways was strong. We checked that in each other, and paradoxically—wrapped up in the other—saw our private despair begin somewhat to recede.

Perseverance is poetry.

Nudging days with little (or catastrophic) failures and fears into some semblance of beauty, of order, is poetry. I will never forget, for instance—in spite of car bombs—a street vendor fashioning pyramids of green-husked almonds in Beirut . . . poetry.

My wife exercised the principle when she asked that I talk to our unborn baby each morning. The baby obviously could not comprehend what I was saying; it was incomprehensible, anyway. But to try in some mysterious way to prepare a soul for entry into the human tragedy so whether arriving head down or feet first the new being could rely on a familiar voice and firm embrace, I began talking to an umbilical cord. And slowly to write poetry again, for its own worth. For life. If we persevere, we preserve.

WAVE

Fans of the oldest living tree,
gold goodbyes fallen on Twentieth Street
in front of the Embassy of Malta.
The street glows, a field of grain
ripe to cut. For days I have been sliding
my shoes through this field,
spinning the fans of ginkgo,
a million Sayonaras, the only gold
standard I know. She said, "Love
sometimes loves so much it must leave."
And she waved all the way up Connecticut
Avenue until her hand was one leaf of ginkgo.
She who came from the wheat fields.

THE SUNKEN ROAD, ANTIETAM 1980

The Sunken Road was now Bloody Lane. Dead Confederates lay so thick there, wrote one Federal soldier, that as far down the road as he could see, a man could have walked upon them without once touching the ground.

—Frederick Tilburg, *Antietam*

Love, take off your bandana.
Spread it along the wall
which once was a picket fence
hung with men from Bloody Lane.

The air above is blue with brain
of the Lord Creator. There is no pain
here. Today is Fourth of July,
a century after the battle cry

went up September 17, 1862, and men
hidden in the cornfield in butternut

and gray were cut like cane by Hooker,
"as closely as could be done with a knife."

Take out our knife and the cheese and drink.
This is not the life or time to fight.
But the air, I know, is brine.
And the 23,000 Blue and Gray who fell

together in the mist that day are suspended.
The war from here turned for the Union.
But our union will not be. Over us, a world
could walk. We are the wounded. Open the wine.

THE ROSE OF BROOKLYN

Another service, roses strewn and acrid.
Another slab of oak waiting for hinges.
Another nail, another drained body—
a flower pulled from the Great Depression,
you were born above the funeral home.

Caskets stopped filling with satin.
The mortician held his stitch
at your scream. His ribs shook
at the life yelling above, the life
that caused the uprights to sag.
A can of powder tumbled onto the satin
and a withered hand. You were not in need
of mascara that prettied the dead
and have never been since. A chandelier
clinked dry tears over the embalmer.

Did you taste the sugared almond
moved across your tongue? That was
your husband to come. Did you feel
the olive oil crossed on the membrane
of your head? Your scream leaped leagues
of ocean, contained cinders of grapes,

and father of cigarettes, father of despair
and father of hope. "We just need water,
and can live in the old ways," he calls,

the candle in his eyes turning a glass to honey.
O suburb more still than the deepest well!
The piano touches a note. Sister grips

blanket; Mother holds couch. Father
in the kitchen alone, cradled in light
in the stable of dark. He writes a cousin

faraway, who is old and filled with gall.
Father makes his own music. He is blessing
water into wine in the pour of cruets of light.

Father in a private pentecost reminding Joe
of age, fissures of the heart
and the length of night. He is doing our work

in the dark. Manufacturer of dresses and loss,
of organdy and ah, felt! Always getting out
his gauze of cheesecloth for there are wounds

abroad and they choose him. He must ask,
why me, as he does his threads together.
Father at the hole-punch machine

putting a place for a garment to breathe
at the underarm. Father remembering vinyl,
remembering choking, brother on brother

and shouts. Father relentless, flipping
the legal pages past law. He is in another room,
beyond lovestruck Sister and wooing piano,

beyond even Mother and her balance. Alone,
writing only what he knows, taking his chance
among curses, guiding the night by hand:

"Admit it. We are all gone wrong. Enchained
to the same rock of pride. Give in to the candles
like St. Blaise. Joe, I know now

when the lights go out, the heart goes out.
Open that machine muscle! Pull the cloth up
from the breastbone, silk of the silkworm,

and shroud yourself like a woman.
Go to the prodigal one. Beat him to centerpoint
where the needle heals. I beg you,

dear cousin, make amends, before the lights
clank on and the candles are useless, when breath
will be short and voile in the air."

A GIFT YOU MUST LOSE

How long before light welds us together?

Palms stand tall in the smog,
old owls at the neck, taller
than little Grandfather
whose clever coal eyes and hands
worked the embroidery machine.
Three years have passed and the palms
are still tall, the smog still burning
the lungs. What has changed
is my chest, wheezing at the sight
of a St. Christopher's medal
hanging in a jeweler's window.

No safety in numbers for Wahib.

In the Damascene Street of Gold
he showed us the sheets from London
no thicker than spacers in a printer's rack,
gold blades too dull to shave with.

Talking pistachios under our nails
we drank dirt coffee, waited patiently
while Wahib, eyes quick and black
as coal, hammered and boiled
the gold, cooked with a desert wind,
coaxing it into *Mary Our Mother*
with a steel needle. This medal

given to Grandfather he gave to me

when we returned to America. Gold burned
into my breastbone the dry
almond village, the no-legged beggar
on the median in Beirut, flies
loving our slaughtered sheep, heaps
of cherries full of worms, the shepherd
flute crooked with blood.
Bright eyes and hands
embroidered with scars
wound around my neck as medal
and not once taken off. Wahib,

Wahib, why did you go off

with your family for a Sunday
by the river? Why is the river
still burning? The tank took no day
off for God and God veered.
The halftrack ground you and your
twin baby girls. Now, they will never
know evil. Only your wife remains
mutilated for her mirror.
And Grandfather? He died breathing
water in the war of his lungs.
He died as you with children around him.

What is there to say now?

Last week at the Pacific
a wave pulled the Mother-in-Gold
over my ears and I dove and dove
for hours. In the gold
surf I dropped to the knees
the sun hammered

it hammered me.

THE AGE OF CRUELTY

Here they pay for their ferocity
—The Inferno, Canto XII

On a September night, a man looks down
into a waste disposal and hears a child
call out. For the first time
in his marriage, he stands still.
For the first time, the disposal speaks to him:
bones, sinew grinding,
ice and flesh made into paste.
His breastbone vibrates.

In the roar a voice is pleading:

They came in the night
with knives, they came with the liberty flame
in their eyes.
The black hole is spinning.
A bone snaps. *In the name of Christ*
the night turned red, in the name of Yahweh
and security. They wanted to own suffering.

Outside, refineries press the bones
of dinosaurs into fuel, render foam
for his beard, Mercurochrome for wounds,

insecticide for the rosebush
cool in the darkness of his window.
"I want to help him," the man says to himself.
"If I do I will lose my hand."

He shuts off the electricity
and searches the hole. No one
is there. Only the teeth.
His hand comes up wet and whole.
Inside, the children and his wife
are caught by a talking, icy light.

Each night when the silence gyrates
the voice below is his alone.
Unless garbage piles up and flies sweep the streets,

America, to survive this age
you will have to lose your hand.

THE BOMB THAT FELL ON ABDU'S FARM

The Phantoms approached, we were told,
like warps in the sky, like gossip
gone real, aimed in steel
at the eyes of the village.

All the farmers and farmers' boys ran
to the rooftops and watched,
for it was terrifying
and beautiful to see a wedge
of silver up from the South.

And they began to fall with a
vengeance, under the anti-air-
craft that ringed Damascus and the
villagers whooped for there seemed
a magic field around their fields.

Until a cow-shed flew in red to the sky.
and a mother milking collapsed
in her milk. The milk ran pink.

Next door, in my great-uncle's newly-
irrigated fields, a bomb fell.
The mud smothered it. The mud
talked to it. The mud wrapped
its death like a mother. And
the bomb with American lettering
did not go off.

Water your gardens always. Always.

JELLYFISH EGGS

For Ei

We wade shin-deep in the channel
emptying into the Chesapeake
and follow it back where the blue crab,
under cover of rushes, sheds his skin
and mates. The sough of the waves
falls behind us. The channel runs quietly
by as we move upstream, parting the water
as a prow of shin. Shadows glide past,
round, turning. You look up
under the bill of your cap.
You have taken the Chesapeake
back into the channel of your eyes.
Part salt, briny, we wade in our blood.
You dip your hand to a rotating shadow
heading toward the sea, and open
your palm to me. There is a clear gel
with imprint of something like a spine.
It was blocking the sun, this clearness,
runner of the warm backwater,
beginning of tendriled fish. Your belly
eclipses the sun, too. Gently, you lay

the clear egg of jelly down into the current
to be the shadow again, the thing of life.
I am glad you did not fling
it into the cattails, though one day
we will be stung. We turn with the channel
into a large pond teeming with minnows,
crabs and spawning jellyfish. To hold
you here and the curled one
is to hold life and to block the sun.
Come back to the sea
where the stingers bob and run.

NAOMI SHIHAB NYE

(1952–)

Naomi Shihab Nye

Born of a Palestinian father and American mother in St. Louis, Missouri, in 1952, Naomi Shihab Nye grew up in Texas, where she graduated from Trinity University in San Antonio. Nye was introduced to the life of a writer early (her father was one of the few Americans of Arab ancestry working as an editor on a major daily newspaper). In addition to her poetic achievements, she is a well-known folksinger in the Southwest, with two record albums already cut (*Lullaby Raft* and *Rutabaga Roo*).

In 1982, Nye was chosen by Josephine Miles for the National Poetry Series with her book *Hugging the Jukebox* (Dutton; republished by Breitenbush). That book and her first, *Different Ways to Pray* (Breitenbush, 1980) both won the Voertman Poetry Prize from the Texas Institute of Letters. *Hugging the Jukebox* was also named to the Notable Books List in 1982 by the American Library Association. Her latest volume of poetry is *Yellow Glove* (Breitenbush, 1986).

Employed since 1974 as a writer-in-the-schools through the Texas Commission on the Arts, Nye has also taught as Holloway Lecturer in Poetry at the University of California, Berkeley, and as poetry lecturer at the University of Texas, Austin. In both 1983 and 1984 Nye traveled abroad for the United States Information Agency's "Arts America" program, giving poetry readings in Pakistan, Bangladesh, Jordan, the West Bank, Syria, Saudi Arabia, the United Arab Emirates and India. In 1966–67 she lived for a year in East Jerusalem with her family.

Nye's poetry has been anthologized in, among others, Edward Field's *A Geography of Poets* and *The Pushcart Prize VII*; it has appeared in the secondary school textbook *Traditions in American Literature* (Scott Foresman & Company).

Nye has modified translations of poetry for PROTA (Project of Translation from Arabic) which appeared in *Modern Arabic Poetry* (Columbia University Press, 1987). She is married to the photographer Michael Nye, and the couple reside with their son in San Antonio, Texas.

"The Gravities of Ancestry"

I began writing poems at age six, after visiting Chicago for the first time. Somehow, seeing faces, streets, and buildings I had never seen before sparked a desire to record the experience, to make witness in words. I have continued writing because nothing else has provided the same discovery, focus, or comfort that writing does.

Being bicultural has always been important to me: even as a child I knew there was more than one way to dress, to eat, to speak, or to think. I felt lucky to have this dual perspective inherent in my parentage, and I was encouraged to explore other ethnic and cultural perspectives as well. Perhaps being bicultural helped me maintain some sense of "otherness" or detachment: while I was growing up in the United States, there was a quiet, old-world part of me which stood back and observed. It took a year's residence among the Arabs and Armenians of Old City Jerusalem to make me feel distinctly American, as well.

The first time I met other Arab American writers, at a conference in Washington, D.C., in 1980, was like a rapturous homecoming. The gravities of ancestry, the camaraderie of familiar images, even a certain slant of humor, were bonds that seemed to connect us. I realized other writers with shared ethnic backgrounds had been celebrating such relationships for a long time.

It seems all writers are engaged in the building of bridges—from their heads to the page, from one page to another, from writer to reader. Maybe bicultural writers who are actively conscious of or interested in heritage build another kind of bridge as well, this one between worlds. But it's not like a bridge, really—it's closer, like a pulse. As I sit here in Texas, pickup truck in the driveway, tortilla factory down the block, my grandmother's West Bank village keeps returning to me. We were there two weeks ago, with the almond trees in fragile white blossom and the unswerving dignity of all those eyes.

MAKING A FIST

We forget that we are all dead men conversing with dead men.
—Jorge Luis Borges

For the first time, on the road north of Tampico,
I felt the life sliding out of me,
a drum in the desert, harder and harder to hear.
I was seven, I lay in the car
watching palm trees swirl a sickening pattern past the glass.
My stomach was a melon split wide inside my skin.

"How do you know if you are going to die?"
I begged my mother.
We had been traveling for days.
With strange confidence she answered,
"When you can no longer make a fist."

Years later I smile to think of that journey,
the borders we must cross separately,
stamped with our unanswerable woes.
I who did not die, who am still living,
still lying in the backseat behind all my questions,
clenching and opening one small hand.

NEGOTIATIONS WITH A VOLCANO

We will call you "Agua" like the rivers and cool jugs.
We will persuade the clouds to nestle around your neck
so you may sleep late.
We would be happy if you slept forever.
We will tend the slopes we plant, singing the songs
our grandfathers taught us before we inherited their fear.
We will try not to argue among ourselves.
When the widow demands extra flour, we will provide it,
remembering the smell of incense on the day of our Lord.

Please think of us as we are, tiny, with skins that burn easily.
Please notice how we have watered the shrubs around our houses
and transplanted the peppers into neat tin cans.
Forgive any anger we feel toward the earth,
when the rains do not come, or they come too much,
and swallow our corn.
It is not easy to be this small and live in your shadow.

Often while we are eating our evening meal
you cross our rooms like a thief,
touching first the radio and then the loom.
Later our dreams begin catching fire around the edges,
they burn like paper, we wake with our hands full of ash.

How can we live like this?
We need to wake and find our shelves intact,
our children slumbering in their quilts.
We need dreams the shape of lakes,
with mornings in them thick as fish.
Shade us while we cast and hook—
but nothing else, nothing else.

THE WHOLE SELF

You put your whole self in
You put your whole self out
Whole self in and you shake it all about
—The Hokey Pokey

When I think of the long history of the self
on its journey to becoming the whole self, I get tired.
It was the kind of trip you keep making,

Over and over again, the bag you pack and repack so often
the shirts start folding themselves the minute
you take them off.

I kept detailed notes in a brown notebook. I could tell you
when the arm joined, when it fell off again,
when the heart found the intended socket and settled down to
pumping.

I could make a map of lost organs, the scrambled liver,
the misplaced brain. Finally finally we met up with one another
on a street corner, in October, during the noon rush.

I could tell you what I was wearing. How suddenly
the face of the harried waitress *made sense*. I gave my order
in a new voice. Spoke the word *vegetables* like a precious code.

Had one relapse at a cowboy dance in Bandera, Texas,
under a sky so fat the full moon
was sitting right on top of us.

Give me back my villages, I moaned,
the ability to touch and remove the hand
without losing anything.

Take me off this mountain where six counties are visible at once.
I want to remember what it felt like, loving by inches.
You put in the whole self—I'll keep with the toe.

But no, it was like telling the eye not to blink.
The self held on to its perimeters, committed forever,
as if the reunion could not be reversed.

I jumped inside the ring, all of me. Dance, then, and I danced,
till the room blurred like water, like blood, *dance*,
and I was leaning headlong into the universe,

Dance! The whole self was a current, a fragile cargo,
a raft someone was paddling through the jungle,
and I was there, waving, and I would be there at the other end.

GOING FOR PEACHES, FREDERICKSBURG, TEXAS

Those with experience look for a special kind.
Red Globe, the skin slips off like a fine silk camisole.
Boy breaks one open with his hands. Yes it's good,
my old relatives say, but we'll look around.
They want me to stop at every peach stand
between Stonewall and Fredericksburg,
leave the air conditioner running,
jump out and ask the price.

Coming up here they talked about
the best ways to die. One favors a plane crash,
but not over a city. One wants to make sure
her grass is watered when she goes.
Ladies, ladies! This peach is fine,
it blushes on both sides.
But they want to keep driving.

In Fredericksburg the houses are stone,
they remind me of wristwatches, glass polished,
years ticking by in each wall.
I don't like stone, says one. What if it fell?
I don't like Fredericksburg, says the other.
Too many Germans driving too slow.
She herself is German as Stuttgart.
The day presses forward, wearing complaints
like charms on its bony wrist.

Actually ladies, (I can't resist),
I don't think you wanted peaches after all,
you just wanted a nip of scenery,
some hills to tuck behind your heads.
The buying starts immediately, from a scarfed woman
who says she gave up teachin' for peachin'.
She has us sign a guest book.

One aunt insists on reloading into her box
to see the fruit on the bottom.
One rejects any slight bruise.
But Ma'am, the seller insists, nature isn't perfect.
Her hands are spotted, like a peach.

On the road, cars weave loose patterns between lanes.
We will float in flowery peach-smell
back to our separate kettles, our private tables
and knives, and line up the bounty,
deciding which ones go where.
A canned peach, says one aunt, lasts ten years.
She was 87 last week. But a frozen peach
tastes better on ice cream.
Everything we have learned so far,
skins alive and ripening, on a day
that was real to us, that was summer,
motion going out and memory coming in.

MY FATHER AND THE FIGTREE

For other fruits my father was indifferent.
He'd point at the cherry trees and say,
"See those? I wish they were figs."
In the evenings he sat by my bed
weaving folktales like vivid little scarves.
They always involved a figtree.
Even when it didn't fit, he'd stick it in.
Once Joha was walking down the road and he saw a figtree.
Or, he tied his camel to a figtree and went to sleep.
Or, later when they caught and arrested him,
his pockets were full of figs.

At age six I ate a dried fig and shrugged.
"That's not what I'm talking about!" he said,
"I'm talking about a fig straight from the earth—
gift of Allah!—on a branch so heavy it touches the ground.

I'm talking about picking the largest fattest sweetest fig
in the world and putting it in my mouth."
(Here he'd stop and close his eyes.)

Years passed, we lived in many houses, none had fig trees.
We had lima beans, zucchini, parsley, beets.
"Plant one!" my mother said, but my father never did.
He tended garden half-heartedly, forgot to water,
let the okra get too big.
"What a dreamer he is. Look how many things he starts
and doesn't finish."

The last time he moved, I got a phone call.
My father, in Arabic, chanting a song I'd never heard.
"What's that?" I said.
"Wait till you see!"
He took me out back to the new yard.
There, in the middle of Dallas, Texas,
a tree with the largest, fattest, sweetest figs in the world.
"It's a figtree song!" he said,
plucking his fruits like ripe tokens,
emblems, assurance
of a world that was always his own.

BLOOD

"A true Arab knows how to catch a fly in his hands,"
my father would say. And he'd prove it,
cupping the buzzer instantly
while the host with the swatter stared.

In the spring our palms peeled like snakes.
True Arabs believed watermelon could heal fifty ways.
I changed these to fit the occasion.

Years before, a girl knocked,
wanted to see the Arab.
I said we didn't have one.

After that my father told me who he was,
"Shihab"—"shooting star"—
a good name, borrowed from the sky.
Once I said, "When we die, we give it back?"
He said that's what a true Arab would say.

Today the headlines clot in my blood.
A little Palestinian dangles a truck on the front page.
Homeless fig, this tragedy with a terrible root
is too big for us. What flag can we wave?
I wave the flag of stone and seed,
table-mat stitched in blue.

I call my father, we talk around the news.
It is too much for him,
neither of his two languages can reach it.
I drive into the country to find sheep, cows,
to plead with the air:
Who calls anyone *civilized*?
Where can the crying heart graze?
What does a true Arab do now?

LUNCH IN NABLUS CITY PARK

When you lunch in a town which has recently known war
under a calm slate sky mirroring none of it,
certain words feel impossible in the mouth.
Casualty: too casual, it must be changed.
A short man stacks mounds of pita bread
on each end of the table, muttering
something about more to come.
Plump birds landing on park benches
surely had their eyes closed recently,
must have seen nothing of weapons or blockades.
When the woman across from you whispers
I don't think we can take it anymore
and you say there are people praying for her

in the mountains of Himalaya and she says
Lady, it is not enough, then what?

A plate of cigar-shaped meatballs, dish of tomato,
friends dipping bread—
I will not marry till there is true love, says one,
throwing back her cascade of perfumed hair.
He says the University of Texas seems remote to him
as Mars, and last month he stayed in his house
for 26 days. He will not leave, he refuses to leave.
In the market they are selling
men's shoes with air-vents, a beggar displays
the giant scab of leg he must drag from alley to alley,
and students gather to discuss what constitutes
genuine protest.

In summers, this cafe is full.
Today only our table sends laughter into the trees.
What cannot be answered checkers the tablecloth
between the squares of white and red.
Where do the souls of hills hide
when there is shooting in the valleys?
What makes a man with a gun seem bigger
than a man with almonds? How can there be war
and the next day eating, a man stacking plates
on the curl of his arm, a table of people
toasting one another in languages of grace:
For you who came so far;
For you who held out, wearing a black scarf
to signify grief;
For you who believe true love can find you
amidst this atlas of tears linking one town
to its own memory of mortar,
when it was still a dream to be built
and people moved here, believing,
and someone with sky and birds in his heart
said this would be a good place for a park.

MY UNCLE MOHAMMED AT MECCA, 1981

This year the wheels of cars
are stronger than the wheels of prayer.
Where were you standing when it hit you,
what blue dome rose up in your heart?

I hold the birds you sent me,
olivewood clumsily carved.
The only thing I have
that you touched.

Why is it so many singulars
attend your name? You lived on one mountain,
sent one gift. You went on one journey
and didn't come home.

We search for the verb
that keeps a man complete.
To resign, to disappear, that's how
I've explained you.

Now I want to believe it was true.
Because you lived apart,
we hold you up. Because no word connected us,
we complete your sentence.

And your house with wind in the windows
instead of curtains
is the house we are building
in the cities of the world.

Uncle of sadness, this is the last pretense:
you understood the world was no pilgrim,
and were brave, and wise,
and wanted to die.

MOTHER OF NOTHING

Sister, the stars have no children.
The stars pecking at each night's darkness
above your trailer would shine back at themselves
in its metal, but they are too far away.
The stones lining your path to the goats
know themselves only as speechless, flat,
gray-in-the-sun.
What begins and ends in the self
without continuance in any other.

You who stand at pre-school fences
watching the endless tumble and slide,
who answer the mothers' Which one is yours?
with blotted murmur and turning away,
listen. Any lack carried
too close to the heart
grows teeth, nibbles off
corners. I heard one say
she had no talent,
another, no time, and there were many
without beauty all those years,
and all of them shrinking.
What sinks to the bottom of the pond
comes up with new colors, or not at all.

We sank, and there was purple,
voluptuous merging of purple and blue,
a new silence living
in the houses of our bodies.
Those who wanted and never received;
who were born without hands,
who had and then lost; the Turkish mother
after the earthquake
with five silent children lined before her,
the women of Beirut

bearing water to their bombed-out rooms,
the fathers in offices
with framed photographs of children on their desks,
and their own private knowledge
of all the hard words.

And we held trees differently
then, and dried plates differently,
because waiting dulls the senses
and when you are no longer waiting,
something wakes up. My cousin said
It's not children, it's a matter of making
life. And I saw the streets opening into the future,
cars passing, mothers with car seats,
children waving out the rear window,
keeping count of all who waved back,
and would we lift our hearts and answer them,
and when we did, what would we say?
And the old preposterous stories of nothing
and everything finally equalling one another
returned in the night. And like relatives,
knew where the secret key was hidden
and let themselves in.

FOR LOST AND FOUND BROTHERS

Where were you in winters of snow,
what ceiling did you stare at
before the dark came home to hold your hand?
What did your mama tell you about the world?

Facts interest me less than the trailing smoke of stories.
Where were you when no one else was there?

You lived in France at the foot of mountains
with paper, with creamy white days.
You hiked railroad tracks dreaming of mirrors,
how one life reflects another, goes back and back and back.

You stood in rooms, your black eyes birds barely landed,
and learned the long river that was your voice.
Thank you, a stone thrown in, a stone quietly sinking.
Thank you, a ripple returned.
So today when you bend to sign the first page of your book
there are other things to thank too,
the days folded behind you, in your wake,
this day connected, more mirrors, more birds.

For you, brothers.
For the blood rivers invisibly harbored.
For the grandfathers who murmured the same songs.
And for the ways we know each other years before meeting,
how strangely and suddenly, on the lonely porches,
in the sleepless mouth of the night,
the sadness drops away, we move forward,
confident we were born into a large family,
our brothers cover the earth.

Elmaz Abinader

(1954–)

Elmaz Abinader

Elmaz Abinader was born in Carmichaels, Pennsylvania, in 1954 of Lebanese immigrant parents. Her father's diaries—he was a trader on the Amazon in the thirties—form the basis of a doctoral dissertation she wrote for the University of Nebraska. She also turned ancestral experiences into a novel, *Stories of Fathers and Sons, Voices of Mothers and Daughters,* written on an Albert Schweitzer Fellowship at the State University of New York at Albany under the tutelage of Toni Morrison, the celebrated novelist.

Abinader has studied under Philip Levine at Columbia University, where she took an MFA degree in creative writing.

Among the many journals in which her poems have appeared are *Nimrod*, *Alaska Quarterly Review*, and *Willow Springs Magazine*. She received First Prize from the Academy of American Poets for her poem "Women of Power Who Write Poetry." Her poems have been anthologized in *All My Grandmothers Could Sing* (Free Rein Press, 1984), a collection of poems by women of Nebraska. A lengthy study of the poetry of Abinader and Naomi Shihab Nye appears in "Starting Anew: Arab American Poetry," by Evelyn Shakir (*Ethnic Forum*, 1983).

Abinader has taught at a number of colleges, including Marymount College and St. Peter's, and is presently teaching English at John Jay College of Criminal Justice in New York City, where she lives with her husband.

"A Way of Thanking"

The need to express what I see in writing is part of an Abinader tradition. For centuries diaries, poems, plays, and stories dramatized the history of the people: public history and private history. Poetry is my way of seeing and measuring myself and my cultures.

I am a poet of an identity, of a concern, of a culture, of a history, and these influence the vision of the poetry. More generally, being an Arab American poet is a political statement that suggests we are, none of us, only writers, but writers whose lives have been fashioned by histories and philosophies and who choose to bring the personal experience of this culture into universal terms in the images we write. Being an Arab American poet is also a gift to my heritage, my only way of thanking my ancestors for my voice, my color, my hair, my parents and siblings, and for the mountains and waters of Lebanon which stay in my memory.

ON A SUMMER NIGHT

The fireflies floated up from the grass.
At the top of the yard, they signalled
to me. I swiped one from the air
and peeked through the cracks of my fingers
to watch its flicker.

I must spend each night alone with my mirrors
around me: books, photographs, pillows,
and an open space. I do not trust
myself in sleep; I will not drop off
into the leisure of a dream. I am the keeper
of this night and its silences.

We lay in the yard and watched the bats
swoop and scream. I could not believe
their blindness as they dove and punched
at the stars. I held my breathing
so they would not hear me.

Sometimes I sit at this window for hours
with a candle behind me in the room.
No bats pass through this sky. It has
no real darkness. And when I see a star,
I watch it disappear through my fingers.

THE GENTRY

It is summer and we sit on the front porch
facing the street. We are the folks who
live in town.

Every day at three, we watch the trail
of piled trucks ascend the hill. When the road shivers,
I stand against the door. Their loads have sheared
the branches of our oaks and chunks of coal
are left behind.

I comfort the trees, stroke their barks.
I pick up a piece of coal. It is clean and shiny
and the ridges are sharp, the surface, smooth.

When the miners come home, some drive past
with their windows open and talk loudly.
The others walk by us alone. We are silent.
With white rings around their eyes, they swing
their silver buckets and call me "miss."

None of the neighbors are miners. They wear gloves
in the garden and lunch with their wives. They do not
keep watch with us. They talk among themselves.
I stand against their fence with my chunk of coal.

DAR A LUZ

(For Schmitz)

The birds fly under the bridge
  swept in the current of the setting sun.
A strip of orange is the last color in the darkening sky.
  Chips of orange are caught on their wings.
We who sit in small apartments have no room for birth.
  We do not break the cold air to walk from the book,
  chair, or quiet phone.
We study languages we'll never use; sing loudly
  until a step is heard at the door.
A streak of color outside the window
  is unnoticed. We examine our faces in the glass.
If we allow the light to pass from our bodies,
  we will go without sleep searching for it.
If we watch the birds go to the bridge,
  we do not follow with the knowledge of the open night.
We close our shutters in silence
  with one slat open and a secret wish.

MAKING IT NEW

My mother hides within folded hands.
A child pushed between each finger.
She sweats tiny prayers, nine days,
and nine days more. They run into years—
even when the breathing stopped,
even when a heart ran down.

I am a body moving past my window,
following each life that dwells
on the edge of my face. I cannot free
myself without cracking a shoulder
or crying aloud. I keep my landscapes dark.

Deep breaths and broken ice. A reaching
back into sleep, where my eyes shut
slowly without words, where each time,
a child is born.

PIGEON ROCK: LEBANON

If I put my hand into the water,
my body would float out and land with the fish
on the coast of Greece, slung against the shore.
In the boat my cousin sings American songs
to please me. He wears high shoes everywhere he goes.

No one was standing on Pigeon Rock
when they showed it to me. The dead lovers might
awaken at night and climb back to the top.
They must live in the caves underneath
and spy on small boats as they pass.

As we walk around the dock, the fishermen
kiss the air and throw up their catch for us.
Fish spill at my feet. My reflections roll
in the stillness of their bloody eyes.
I tried to hold one but couldn't. It dropped
into the net where no lovers' bodies lie.

LETTERS FROM HOME

To My Father

Everytime you weep, I feel the surface
of a river somewhere on earth is breaking.
You wipe your eyes as you read aloud
a letter from the old country. From the floor
I watch the curls of the words through the sheer
pages. Your brothers and sisters have gathered
around you. I don't understand the language
but feel a single breath of grief holding this room.

Your mother tells of her weakening body.
She walks to church but cannot leave
the village. When you sat with her,
I recognized the common colors of your skins.
You wanted her forgiveness for your absence
but did not ask. She took you to her closet
to show you the linens she had gathered which
have already yellowed. Her hands seemed small
through the lace. She did not understand
why you hugged her shoulders.

She tells you of the refuge people have found
in the village. Others have gone to Paris.
You have a niece who is a doctor, a nephew,
an architect. Your own children seem like nomads.
They sit in scattered apartments where you can't
see your three daughters gazing from their windows.
Or your three sons pacing the old wood of their rooms,
yet you write to your mother, they still pray.

You visit your mother now when you can.
Each summer you cross the Mediterranean;
each summer you stand behind her house
looking into the sea, hoping she does not die
this time. And when these letters come, I run
my fingers across the pages. I hope I can learn
the languages you have come to know.

NOTES

AMEEN RIHANI

''In Loafing''

Al-Fared (Ibn al-Farid): Born in 1182, the son of a Cairo notary, al-Farid lived the life of a Sufi poet. After his death in 1235 he was buried at the foot of the Muqattam hills.

Jelal ^{c}ud-Deen Rumy (Jelal al-Din Rumi): considered by many to be the greatest mystic poet in Islam, and perhaps the greatest in any language (he wrote in Persian). Born in Balkh (present-day Afghanistan) in 1207, Rumi led the quiet life of a religious teacher in Konya (Turkey) until age thirty-seven when he came under the influence of a wandering dervish, Shams al-Din. To symbolize the search for the lost Divine Beloved, represented by a departed Shams al-Din, Rumi invented the famous circle dance of the Mevlevi whirling dervishes. In the heat of the dance he would extemporaneously speak poetry which was recorded by followers. He died in 1272.

''I Dreamt I Was a Donkey-Boy Again''

Mulayiah (mawlay): my master.

Salaam: peace.

Bulbul: a songbird thought to be a nightingale, often mentioned in Arabic poetry.

''Gibran''

A young Gibran met the older Rihani in New York when the latter's work was being published and lauded. They were wary friends for a time; a friend of Mary Haskell and Gibran, Charlotte Teller, became involved with Rihani.

Jubail: ancient Byblos (which derives from the Greek word for "book," hence "bible") is today a small fishing village between Beirut and Tripoli, Lebanon. In ancient times it was a source of papyrus and a port for the cedar trade.

Tammuz: an early Mesopotamian god of fertility, gored by a wild boar in Mount Lebanon, whose blood was said to restore life to vegetation (spring) and cause the Nahr (River) Ibrahim to flow red (geologists pointed to its red soil). Tammuz' love is Ishtar, who brought him back from the dead. According to Philip Hitti, "Wild with joy on his restoration, Byblian women sacrificed their virginity at Ishtar's temple." The Phoenicians carried the Tammuz-Ishtar cult throughout the Mediterranean basin.

Quais (Imri'u al-Qays): the greatest of the pre-Islamic desert poets, so judged by the prophet Mohammed.

al-Ma^{c}arri (Abu al-Ala al-Ma^{c}arri): one of the great skeptic poets in Arabic literature and something of a celebrated anomaly in the entire tradition. Born in Ma^{c}arrah, Syria, in A.D. 973, he was blind by the age of four. He lived an ascetic, vegetarian existence, and scorned religious institutions, saying, "My aim is to speak the truth." Al-Ma^{c}arri was a strong influence on Gibran and Rihani, as well as on many contemporary Arab poets.

"Lilatu Laili"

Lilatu laili (laylatu al-layali): the most splendid of nights, literally, the night of nights.

Laila (Layla): the lover of Qays (see above). Their story in Arabic lore is the equivalent of the Romeo and Juliet tale.

"Constantinople"

Othman: founder of the Ottoman Empire.

Paleologue: a coined term derived from *palaeologian*, or one who rests on the authority of antiquity.

"A Chant of Mystics"

Sana'i (Sana'y): Persian Sufi poet.

Attar: Farid ud-Din Abu Hamid Mohammed ben Ibrahim, called Attar, or "perfumer" (1120–1230). A Persian Sufi poet from Nishapur who wrote *The Conference of the Birds*. Legend says Attar was killed by a soldier of Genghis Khan. Rumi said of him, "Attar is the soul itself."

'Arabi: a Spanish Arab from Seville, Muhyi al-Din ibn 'Arabi (1165–1240), was called by Hitti "the greatest mystic the Arabs produced and one of their greatest poets."

Rabi^{c}a (Rabi^{c}ah al-^{c}Adawiyyah): a Sufi woman born in Basrah, Iraq, sold into slavery, released by her master when he noticed a radiance around her head; the first saint of Islam, who once said, "My love of Allah leaves no room for hating Satan."

Gazzali: Abu Hami Muhammah al-Ghazali (1058–1111), a Persian Sufi mystic who, after suffering a nervous breakdown at age thirty-nine, retreated from public and family life, wandering until taking refugee in a minaret at the Omayyad mosque in Damascus; considered the greatest theologian in Islam and a legitimizer of Sufism in the tradition. He was mentioned by Dante, and his teachings influenced Thomas Aquinas and Maimonedes.

Hallaj: a Persian Sufi mystic who followed the example of Jesus, saying "I am the Truth"; an ecstatic monist who, on the way to being crucified in Baghdad in A.D. 922, forgave his tormentors in Christlike fashion.

Jelal ^{c}ud-Din Rumi: see notes for "In Loafing."

Fared: see notes for "In Loafing."

KAHLIL GIBRAN

"Poets and Poems"

Al-Mutanabbi (A.D. 915–65): a poet of the classical age of Islam, considered by many Arabs to be their finest poet; called by Omar Pound "probably the most difficult important poet for a Westerner to appreciate." He was killed by marauders on returning to Baghdad from Persia.

Al-Farid: See notes for Ameen Rihani, "In Loafing."

Al Maary: See notes for Ameen Rihani, "Gibran."

"Defeat"

The poem was published as a pamphlet predating publication of *The Madman*. Hopeful of rallying American support against the Ottoman Turkish empire, "Defeat" was also sent to cheer the Serbian rebels at Kossovo during the First World War.

"Kahlil the Heretic":

read in June 1987 at the presentation of a Gibran plaque to Mayor Raymond Flynn of Boston before a crowd of 1,000; appeared in the Arabic *al-Arwah al-Mutamarridah* (1909) and was translated into English by H. M. Nahmad as part of *Spirits Rebellious* (1948). Suhail Bushrui translated a section of this well-known tale into poetic form for a thin commemorative volume he edited in Beirut, *An Introduction to Kahlil Gibran*. His version is ours.

Durzi: belonging to the Druze, a schismatic Shiite Muslim sect whose members live chiefly in Lebanon and Syria, with a few in Israel.

Shi^{c}i: belonging to the Shi^{c}ah sect, the major Islamic sect after the Sunni, called thus because Shiites were originally *Shi^{c}ah*, or partisans of Ali (d. A.D. 661), the prophet Mohammed's first cousin and husband of his only surviving daughter, Fatimah. The mystical strain in Islam tends to come from the Shiites. Their largest concentration is in Iran, and they make up approximately half of Iraq's population. Recently Shiites have become the largest religious sect in Lebanon, and there are scattered Shiite communities throughout the Arabian peninsula.

Sunni: belonging to the Sunni or "orthodox" Islamic sect, so called after the *sunna*, or lifestyle and rules of conduct of the prophet Mohammed. The great majority of Muslims are Sunnis.

"The Fox"

Khalil Hawi, the eminent Lebanese poet and Gibran critic, relates the poem to Lebanese folklore. Gibran read this poem on meeting the great Mexican painter Jose Orozco, who enjoyed it and became a friend.

"Dead Are My People"

written in 1916 while 100,000—one quarter of the population—were dying of starvation in Lebanon. France and Britain had blockaded the Lebanese coast to squeeze the Ottomans during the First World War, and with Turkish soldiers confiscating wheat and other foodstuffs, the native population had virtually nothing to eat for four years. The poem appeared originally in the special famine issue of *al-Funoon*, October 1916.

"The Sufi"

apparently Gibran's last poem, unpublished in a collection until this translation by Andrew Ghareeb, written two months before his death. It appears in another English version in the archives of Mary Haskell, but was written originally in Arabic.

"The Gravedigger"

first published in *Mirat al-Gharb* (New York) in the spring of 1913, and later in Gibran's collection *al-^{c}Awasif* (Cairo, 1920). Mary Haskell noted in her journal on April 6, 1913, that the poem was being "widely quoted as nonsense, madness, meaningless—parodied very cleverly, and admired." Writing it in a feverish summer, 1912, Gibran told her, "It is the best thing I've done yet." A translation of the work appears as prose in *A Treasury of Kahlil Gibran*, with omissions. It does not, for example, even mention the speaker's divorce. The Ghareeb translation is previously unpublished.

Abdullah (^{c}Abdullah): a common Muslim and Arab name meaning God's slave.

Djinns: plural of djinn, also spelled jinn or jinni (genie derives from it); creatures that inhabit the earth occupy a middle range between humans and spirits, and have supernatural powers.

JAMIL HOLWAY

"Throbbings"

Zaynab: a common Arab female name.

ELIA MADEY (ABU MADI)

"Riddles"

Leyla: See Laila in notes for Ameen Rihani, "Lilatu Laili."

Ibn-ul-Mullawah: Qays Ibn al-Mulawwah, Layla's lover (see notes for Ameen Rihani, "I Dreamt I Was a Donkey Boy Again" and "Lilatu Laili").

ETEL ADNAN

"The Beirut-Hell Express"

Written in 1970, in many ways the poem foretells the Lebanese Civil War, which began in 1975 and continues to this day.

Ouranos: the planet Uranus. Ouranus is the Arabic pronunciation. In Greek mythology Uranus is the sky personified as a god.

Queen Zenobia: third-century Nabatean queen of Palmyra, Syria, who also ruled over Egypt and Anatolia and defied the Roman empire. She was captured in A.D. 272 after a long, harrowing siege of the city by the Romans, but killed herself with a poisoned ring rather than submit to the humiliation of captivity. She is viewed by Arabs as a heroine who challenged foreign conquerors.

Fouad Gabriel Naffah: contemporary Lebanese poet (1925–79) who wrote in French and lived in poverty.

Tammouz (Tammuz): See notes for Ameen Rihani, "Gibran."

A. U. B.: the American University of Beirut, Lebanon.

Wahdat Camp: a major Palestinian refugee camp in Amman, Jordan, that was a stronghold for guerrillas in the 1970 clashes between Palestinian forces and the Jordanian army known as Black September.

Mount Sannine (Sannin): a snow-capped Lebanese mountain.

Al-Ghazali (al-Ghazali): See notes for Ameen Rihani, "A Chant of Mystics."

Irbid: a city in northern Jordan.

Zarka (al-Zarqa'): a Jordanian city.

Ur: an ancient city in Iraq.

Basrah: an Iraqi port city at the confluence of the Tigris and Euphrates rivers.

"Journey to Mount Tamalpais"

Errynies: malevolent Greek goddesses of wind.

D. H. MELHEM

"Some Notes on Origins"

Oud (ʿud): lute.

Durbakkah: bongo drum.

"To an Ethiopian Child"

Korareema: Amharic, Ethiopian spice.

Sansevieria: genus of African or Asian herbs; leaves sometimes used in making bowstrings, cordage, or in packing.

Shehma: Amharic, Ethiopian national cotton dress.

Kosso tree: Ethiopian tree whose fruit had medicinal uses.

Baga: Amharic, Ethiopian dry season (summer, September–May).

Keuramt: Amharic, Ethiopian rainy season (winter, June–August).

"Rest in Love"

Georgette Deyratani: Melham: the poet's mother, who actually authored the last entry in this poetic cycle (on Ellis Island).

SAMUEL HAZO

"For Fawzi in Jerusalem"

Jerash: an ancient Roman city in Jordan.

Jericho: a town on the West Bank at the Jordan River; considered one of the most ancient cities in history, if not *the* most ancient; site of several biblical stories including that of Joshua blowing down Jericho's walls with a ram's horn. The city was ringed by three Palestinian refugee camps after 1948, two of which were bulldozed by the Israel army in 1985.

EUGENE PAUL NASSAR

"East Utica"

Oof (awf): a sound used sometimes as a refrain in Arab singing, especially in folk songs. The exact emotional connotation (sadness or pleasure) depends on the context. The audience may interrupt the singer with the same sound to express approval or joy.

Mount Sunnin: See notes for Etel Adnan, "The Beirut-Hell Express."

St. Maron: an ascetic monk who preached in the wilderness northeast of Antioch in the fifth century A.D.; his followers later took refuge in Mount Lebanon and began the Maronite rite of the Catholic church. There are at least 600,000 Maronites in Lebanon today, and 51,000 practicing Maronites in the United States.

Khreibe (ghrabi): a butter cookie sometimes topped with pistachios or almonds.

Bitlawa (baqlawah): an Arabic sweet, often diamond-shaped, stuffed with pistachios or walnuts and topped with attar, or orange-water syrup.

"A Disputation with Kahlil Gibran"

Wadi Qadischa: the Qadisha valley which contains a precipitous gorge high in the Lebanese mountains through which the Qadisha (holy) river flows from its source in a cedar grove; the founding spot of the Maronite sect where a monastery is carved into rock; Kahlil Gibran's hometown of Bsharri is located here.

Quoddous: prayer before Communion in the Maronite rite's Mass:

> Quoddous, quoddous, quoddous.
> Rabbou Sabaouth
> Assama wul ard memlouatanee
> min majdeka latheem (or:
> Qudus, qudus, qudus
> Rabbu Sab^{c}auth
> Al-sama' wa al-ard mamlu' atayni
> min majdik al-^{c}athim)

Saidanaya (Sidnaya): "Our Lady" in Aramaic, but also "hunting places" after the Byzantine Emperor Justinian had a vision in A.D. 547 while out hunting gazelles; the Emperor constructed a church on the spot of the vision, about twenty miles east of Damascus. Sidnaya today is a miraculous site of Eastern Christianity similar to Lourdes in the West.

Melkites: from *malek*, or king; Syrian Christians belonging to a Byzantine rite who became known as Melkites (or royalists) in the seventh century. In 1724, they detached themselves from Eastern Orthodoxy and allied with Rome; sometimes called "Greek Catholics." There are about 300,000 Melkites in Lebanon today (many in Zahle), and 25,000 active in the United States.

H. S. (SAM) HAMOD

"Lines to My Father"

Kib'be (kibbah): Arabic, especially Lebanese and Syrian, dish made from bulgur (cracked wheat) and minced meat; individual pieces are egg- or diamond-shaped.

"After the Funeral of Assam Hamady"

Hysht Iyat (laysh bit^c^ayyit): why are you crying? in colloquial Lebanese Arabic

Shu bikkee (shu biki): "What's the matter with you?" in colloquial Lebanese Arabic

Sullee (salli): pray.

Allahu Ahkbar
Ash haduu n lah illah illilawhh
Muhammed rasoul illawh
(Allahu akbar
Ashhadu anna la ilaha illa allah
Muhammadun rasolu allah): The muslim call to prayer, translated as—God is Great, I witness that there is no God but Allah and Muhammad is His Messenger.

Bishmee lahee
a rah'manee raheem
malik a youm a deen
ehde nuseerota el mustakeem
seyrota la theena
en umta ailiy him
ghyrug mugthubee aliy him
willathouu leen
(Bismi allahi al-rahman al-rahim
maliki yawmi al-din
Ihdina al-sirata al-mustaqim
sirata allathina
an^c^amta ^c^a layhim
ghayru al-maghdubi ^c^alayhim
wala al-dallin):

Parts of the opening prayer of the Quran, al-Fatihah, first prayer said before all prayers. It is analagous in its use by Muslims to the Lord's Prayer for Christians; translated by A. J. Arberry as—In the Name of God, the Merciful, the Compassionate. Praise belongs to God, the Lord of all Being, the all-merciful, the all compassionate, the Master of the Day of Doom. Thee only do we serve; to Thee alone we pray for succour. Guide us in the straight path, the path of those whom Thou hast blessed, not of those against whom Thou art wrathful, nor of those who are astray.

Bishmee lahee
a rah'maneel raheem
khul waha lahu uhud
Allahu sumud

lum yuulud wa'alum uulud
walum yakun a kuf one uhud
willa thouu leen. Ameen.
(Bismi allahi al-rahman al-rahim
qul huwa allahu ahad
allahu al-samad
lam yalid wa lam yulad
wa lam yakun lahu Kufu'an ahad
wa la al-dallin
Amin):

Parts of the Sura al-Samad (or Unity/Source), translated by Thomas Irving as—In the Name of God, The Merciful, the Compassionate,
Say God is Unique,
God is the Source.
He has not fathered anyone, nor has He fathered.
And there is nothing comparable to Him.
. . . nor of those who are astray.
Amen.

"Dying with the Wrong Name"

Jezzine: a town in southern Lebanon.

Im'a Brahim (Um Ibrahim): mother of Abraham

Fatiyah (fatayir): meat or spinach pies.

Asalamu Aleikum (al-salamu ᶜalaykum): peace be with you; the primary Arab greeting.

"Libyan/Egyptian Acrobats/Israeli Air Circus"

On February 21, 1973, the Israeli air force shot down a Libyan passenger jet, killing 108 civilians.

JACK MARSHALL

"The United Way" Rezi: Charles Reznikoff, American poet (1894–1976).

FAWAZ TURKI

"In Search of Yacove Eved"

Salaam/Shalom: peace, in Arabic and Hebrew, respectively.

Shaaer (shaᶜir): Arabic for poet.

"Tel Zaatar Was the Hill of Thyme"

It is the duty of every Lebanese to kill one Palestinian: statement attributed to Abu Arz, leader of the Guardians of the Cedar, an ultra-right-wing Christian faction in Lebanon; the phrase has been scrawled on Beirut walls since the start of the civil war in 1975.

Bloody April 1948: On April 9, 1948, the Irgun gang, led by Menachem Begin, massacred between 116 and 250 Palestinians in the village of Deir Yassin.

Helpless June 1967: when the Egyptian, Syrian, and Jordanian armies were stunningly defeated in six days by the Israeli army; referred to as the June War, or Six-Day War.

Allenby Bridge: a bridge over the Jordan River which connects the West Bank and Jordan, named for a British general who fought against the Turks in World War I.

Black September 1970: In clashes between the Palestinian guerrillas and Jordanian army, the army killed an estimated 5,000–20,000 Palestinians and effectively expelled the guerrillas from Jordan.

Izz el Deen el Kassam (ʿIz al-Din al-Qassam): a Palestinian peasant leader of the 1936 popular revolt against the British; he was killed by the British that same year.

Karameh: a refugee camp on the border of the West Bank and Jordan where the emerging Palestinian *feda'yyin* forces fought a credible pitched battle against the Israeli army in 1968.

SHARIF S. ELMUSA

"Father Lullabies the Unborn"

Albi ala . . . : an Arabic proverb.

NAOMI SHIHAB NYE

"My Father and the Figtree"

Joha (Juha): a comic figure in Arabic folklore. He appears as a fictional character, Nasr al-Din, which the Sufis employ in their parables for instruction in the Sufi method. These parables are often ingenious with unanticipated, humorously ironic endings.

"Lunch in Nablus City Park"

Nablus: a major West Bank town.

blockaded veins, and tongues that stung
in English. Your scream was neither
English nor Arabic, but life
out of a funeral home, tears
more abundant than chandeliers, skin
pure as the snows of Lebanon, and though
you were blind you would see
with eyes shined like onyx, you would wake
the living from their hate with a cry
that could crack
or sing your wheezing son to sleep.

Not a tree, but a rose
bloomed in Brooklyn
in our first home, and our last.

MY FATHER WRITING JOE HAMRAH IN A BLACKOUT

Candles of my father, protect the page.
The refrigerator's out, and so's the age.
The streets lament in pitch. He writes

beyond hope and wage in a kitchen
where we just broke bread. Dread
on his mind? More the unstitching of darkness

as Sister curls with blanket, listening
to piano of her boyfriend. Mother sits near,
mesmerized by Mendelssohn. But it is

as if the music comes from candlepower,
the power of flame and of night. Father's
begun, *Introibo ad altare Dei*, on a legal pad

between two tall tongues. Father of candles,
father of pens, father of debits,
father of credits, father of ikons

ACKNOWLEDGMENTS AND CREDITS

AMEEN RIHANI. "In Loafing," "I Dreamt I Was a Donkey Boy Again," reprinted from *The Book of Khalid* by Ameen Rihani, copyright 1911, Dodd, Mead; "It Was All for Him," "Lilatu Lailu," from *Myrtle and Myrrh*, by Ameen Rihani, copyright 1905 The Gorham Press, and reprinted by The Rihani House, Beirut, 1955, reprinted by permission of the publishers; excerpt from "Gibran" from *Hutaf al Awdiah* (*Call of the Valleys*), The Rihani House, 1955; "Constantinople," excerpt from "The Fugitive," excerpts from "A Chant of Mystics," from *A Chant of Mystics and Other Poems* by Ameen Rihani, copyright 1921 James T. White and Co., and reprinted by The Rihani House, Beirut, 1970, reprinted by permission of the publishers.

KAHLIL GIBRAN. "Poets and Poems" from *A Second Treasury of Kahlil Gibran* by Kahlil Gibran, translated by Anthony Rizcallah Ferris, copyright 1962 The Citadel Press, reprinted by permission of the publishers; "The Madman" Prologue, "Defeat," and "The Fox" from *The Madman, His Parables and Poems* by Kahlil Gibran, copyright 1918 by Kahlil Gibran and renewed 1946 by Comite National de Gibran, reprinted by permission of Alfred A. Knopf, Inc.; excerpt from "Kahlil the Heretic" from *An Introduction to Kahlil Gibran* by Suheil Bushrui, Dar El Mashreq, 1970, reprinted by permission of the author; "Mary Magdalen," "A Cobbler in Jerusalem," "Mannus the Pompeiian to a Greek" from *Jesus the Son of Man* by Kahlil Gibran, copyright 1928 by Kahlil Gibran and renewed 1956 by Administrators CTA of Kahlil Gibran Estate and Mary Gibran, reprinted by permission of Alfred A. Knopf, Inc.; "Heavy-laden Is My Soul" from

The Garden of the Prophet by Kahlil Gibran, copyright 1933 by Kahlil Gibran and renewed 1961 by Mary G. Gibran, reprinted by permission of Alfred A. Knopf, Inc.; "Love" from *The Forerunner* by Kahlil Gibran, copyright 1920 by Kahlil Gibran and renewed 1948 by Administrators CTA of Kahlil Gibran Estate and Mary Gibran, reprinted by permission of Alfred A. Knopf, Inc.; "Song of the Wave" from *A Tear and a Smile* by Kahlil Gibran, translated by H. M. Nahmad, copyright 1950 by Alfred A. Knopf, Inc., reprinted by permission of Alfred A. Knopf, Inc.; excerpt from "My Soul Counselled Me" from *Prose Poems* by Kahlil Gibran, translated by Andrew Ghareeb, copyright 1934 and renewed 1962 by Alfred A. Knopf, Inc., reprinted by permission of Alfred A. Knopf, Inc.; "Dead Are My People" from *A Treasury of Kahlil Gibran* by Kahlil Gibran, translated by Anthony Rizcallah Ferris, copyright 1947 The Citadel Press (Lyle Stuart), reprinted by permission of the publisher; "The Two Poems" from *The Wanderer: His Parables and His Sayings* by Kahlil Gibran, copyright 1932 by Alfred A. Knopf, Inc., and renewed 1960 by Mary G. Gibran, reprinted by permission of Alfred A. Knopf, Inc.

JAMIL HOLWAY. "Satan" and "Throbbings" from *Arab Perspectives*, March 1984, reprinted by permission of the translator.

MIKHAIL NAIMY. "A Solemn Vow" from *The New York Times*, April 1, 1928; "Hunger" from *The New York Times*, August 30, 1930, copyright 1928–30 by The New York Times Company, reprinted by permission; the selection from al-Sabᶜun and "Close Your Eyes and See," from *A New Year: Stories, Autobiography and Poems* (Leiden: E. J. Brill, 1974), translated by J. R. Perry, reprinted by permission of the publisher.

ELIA ABU MADI. "The Silent Tear" from *Arab Perspectives*, October 1983, reprinted by permission of the translator; "Riddles" appeared in slightly different form in the *Springfield Republican*, April 1929, and in *Syrian World*, April 1929, reprinted by permission of the translator.

ETEL ADNAN. "The Beirut-Hell Express," from *Women of the Fertile Crescent, Modern Poetry by Arab Women*, edited by Kamal

Boullata, Three Continents Press, 1978, translated by the author from *L'express Beyrouth-Enfer* (Paris, 1973), reprinted by permission of the author, excerpt from *Journey to Mount Tamalpais* by Etel Adnan, copyright 1986, The Post-Apollo Press, Simone Fattal, publisher, reprinted by permission of the author.

D. H. MELHEM. "lamentation after jeremiah to exorcise high rental/ high rise building scheduled for construction with public funds" from *Notes on 94th Street* by D.H. Melhem, Dovetail Press, 1972, reprinted by permission of the author; "Grandfather: Frailty Is Not the Story" from *East Hampton Star*, May 1, 1986, reprinted by permission of the author; "To an Ethiopian Child," from *Poets for Africa: An International Anthology for Hunger Relief*, 1986, reprinted by permission of the author; excerpts from *Rest in Love*, Dovetail Press, 1975, reprinted by permission of the author.

SAMUEL HAZO. "The Toys," "Only the New Branches Bloom," "Maps for a Son are Drawn As You Go," "Some Words for President Wilson," by Samuel Hazo, from *To Paris*. Copyright © 1974, 1976, 1978, 1980, 1981 by Samuel Hazo. Reprinted by permission of New Directions Publishing Corp. "Pittsburgh in Passing," "The Drenching," "Child of Our Bodies," "For Fawzi in Jerusalem," "To My Mother," from *Once for the Last Bandit, New and Previous Poems* by Samuel Hazo, copyright © 1972 University of Pittsburgh Press, reprinted by permission of the author; "The World that Lightning Makes," from *And Not Surrender, American Poets in Lebanon*, copyright © 1982 Arab American Cultural Foundation, reprinted by permission of the author; "Silence Spoken Here," from *The First and Only Sailing*, Arab American Cultural Foundation, 1981, reprinted by permission of the author.

JOSEPH AWAD. "The Man Who Loved Flamenco," "I Think Continually of Those Who Were True Failures," "Generations," "First Snow," from *The Neon Distances* by Joseph Awad, copyright 1980 Joseph Awad, The Golden Quill Press, reprinted by permission of the author; "The Widower" from *The Lyric*, reprinted by permission of the author, "For Jude's Lebanon," from *The Small Pond Review*,

1985, reprinted by permission of the editor; "Variations on a Theme" from *Parnassus*, reprinted by permission of the author.

EUGENE PAUL NASSAR. Excerpts from "East Utica" and "A Disputation with Kahlil Gibran" from *Wind of the Land* by Eugene Paul Nassar, Association of Arab American University Graduates, copyright 1978 Eugene Paul Nassar, reprinted by permission of the author.

H. S. (SAM) HAMOD. "Lines to My Father," "After the Funeral of Assam Hamady," "Dying with the Wrong Name," "Letter," "Leaves," "Libyan/Egyptian Acrobats/Israeli Air Circus," excerpt from "Moving," from *Dying with the Wrong Name, New and Selected Poems 1968–1979* by Sam Hamod, Anthe Publications, copyright 1980 Sam Hamod, reprinted by permission of the author.

JACK MARSHALL. "Thirty-Seven," "Letter to My Father on the Other Side," "The United Way," "The Months of Love," from *Arabian Nights* by Jack Marshall, Coffee House Press, copyright 1986 Jack Marshall, reprinted by permission of the author; "Still," from *Arriving on the Playing Fields of Paradise* by Jack Marshall, Jazz Press, copyright 1984 Jack Marshall, reprinted by permission of the author.

FAWAZ TURKI. "In Search of Yacove Eved," "Moments of Ridicule and Love," "Being a Good *Americani*," excerpt from "Tel Zaatar Was the Hill of Thyme," from *Tel Zaatar Was the Hill of Thyme* by Fawaz Turki, Palestine Review Press, copyright 1978 Fawaz Turki, reprinted by permission of the author.

DORIS SAFIE. "In the Middle of Reading One More Poem With Brueghel as a Metaphor," from *Cedar Rock*, Fall 1984, reprinted by permission of the author.

BEN BENNANI. "Letters to Lebanon" appeared in somewhat different form as "Letters to My Mother" in *A Bowl of Sorrow* by B. M. Bennani, Greenfield Review Press, copyright 1971 B. M. Bennani, reprinted by permission of the author; "Camel's Bite" from *Camel's*

Bite by Ben Bennani, Jelm Mountain Press, copyright 1980 Ben Bennani, reprinted by permission of the author.

SHARIF S. ELMUSA. "She Fans the Word," from the *Christian Science Monitor*, copyright 1986, reprinted by permission of the author; "The Two Angels," "Expatriates," from *Cedar Rock*, Spring 1984; "Bookishness" from *Visions*, 1986; "Snapshots" from *The Greenfield Review*, 1985; "In the Refugee Camp" from *Poetry East*, Winter, 1988—reprinted by permission of the author.

LAWRENCE JOSEPH. "Curriculum Vitae," "Sand Nigger," "That's All," reprinted from *Curriculum Vitae*, by Lawrence Joseph, by permission of the University of Pittsburgh Press, copyright 1988 by Lawrence Joseph; "Then," "Not Yet," "It's Not Me Shouting at No One," reprinted from *Shouting at No One*, by Lawrence Joseph, by permission of the University of Pittsburgh Press, copyright 1983 by Lawrence Joseph.

GREGORY ORFALEA. "Wave," "The Sunken Road, Antietam 1980," "The Rose of Brooklyn," "My Father Writing Joe Hamrah in a Blackout," "A Gift You Must Lose," "The Age of Cruelty," "The Bomb That Fell on Abdou's Farm," "Jellyfish Eggs," from *The Capital of Solitude* by Gregory Orfalea, Ithaca House, copyright 1988 Gregory Orfalea, reprinted by permission of the author.

NAOMI SHIHAB NYE. "Making a Fist," "For Lost and Found Brothers," from *Hugging the Jukebox* by Naomi Shihab Nye, E.P. Dutton, copyright 1982 Naomi Shihab Nye (reprinted by Breitenbush Books, 1984), reprinted by permission of the author; "Negotiations with a Volcano," "The Whole Self," "My Father and the Figtree," from *Different Ways to Pray* by Naomi Shihab Nye, Breitenbush Publications, copyright 1980 Naomi Shihab Nye, reprinted by permission of the author; "Going for Peaches, Fredericksburg, Texas," "Blood," "Lunch in Nablus City Park," "My Uncle Mohammed at Mecca, 1981," "Mother of Nothing," from *Yellow Glove* by Naomi Shihab Nye, Breitenbush Books, copyright 1986 Naomi Shihab Nye, reprinted by permission of the author.

ELMAZ ABINADER. "Making It New" from *Nimrod*, Fall/Winter 1981, reprinted by permission of the author; "Pigeon Rock: Lebanon" from *Amelia*, April 1985, reprinted by permission of the author; "Letters from Home" from *Wrapping the Grapeleaves, A Sheaf of Arab American Poetry*, copyright 1982 Arab American Anti-Discrimination Committee, reprinted by permission of the author.

Of related interest

On Entering the Sea

The Erotic and Other Poetry of Nizar Qabbani

Translated from the Arabic by Lena Jayyusi and Sharif Elmusa with Jack Collum, Diana Der Hovanessian, W. S. Merwin, Christopher Middleton, Naomi Shihab Nye, Jeremy Reed and John Heath-Stubbs

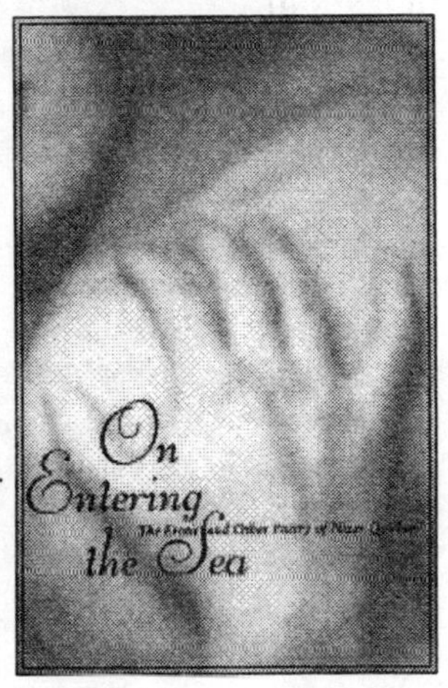

"... one of the greatest love poets of all time... Whether he's writing of love or war, Qabbani achieves a mythic dimension... [a] beautiful collection..."

—Booklist

"... a generous selection of the work of an important poet in Arabic to the English-speaking world... Qabbani's poems of exile and elegy are especially deeply felt, and he is a poet of subtle intelligence."

—Library Journal

In a political age, in which the struggle against external and internal oppression has become central in Arabic poetry, Nizar Qabbani has succeeded in re-establishing the vitality and perennial force of the erotic in human life. Picking up a tradition of Arabic love poetry sixteen centuries old, he has enriched it with the experience of a modern man deeply aware of the changing status of women in contemporary times, and given the most eloquent poetic expression to the imperative of women's freedom and her right to assume control over her body and emotions.

An accomplished master of the erotic, standing among the best love poets in the world, Qabbani has asserted life and joy in the face of chaos and tragedy, paying fervent homage, sustained over five decades, to woman's grace and loveliness. As such he has been able to bring equilibrium and decorum to a poetry in crisis, reviving faith in the possibility of happiness and emotional fulfillment. Yet he is also moved to anger by the forces of evil around him, and the opposing poles of exaltation and rage, of agony and ecstasy, describe his unique experiment.

Nizar Qabbani was born in Damascus in 1923. He is the author of over 50 collections of poetry and is the recipient of numerous literary awards.

Poetry • 6" x 9" • 208 pages
ISBN 1-56656-186-8 — $22.95 hb • ISBN 1-56656-193-0 — $15.00 pb
add $5.00 shipping and handling • MA residents also add 5% sales tax

To order or request our complete catalog,
please call us at **1-800-238-LINK** or write to:
Interlink Publishing
46 Crosby Street, Northampton, MA 01060
e-mail: interpg@aol.com • website: www.interlinkbooks.com

EMERGING VOICES

⌘ NEW INTERNATIONAL FICTION SERIES ⌘

The best way to learn about people and places far away

This series is designed to bring North American readers the once-unheard voices of writers who have achieved wide acclaim at home, but have not been recognized beyond the borders of their native lands. It publishes the best of the world's contemporary literature in translation and original English.

from Syria

Sabriya

Damascus Bitter Sweet

by Ulfat Idilbi

trans. by P. Clark

"*Sabriya* is a haunting, accomplished novel about the lives of women in the 1920's Syria... Idilbi's stately prose is relentless in its exposure of Sabriya's despair... [This novel] reveals Ulfat Idilbi as the possessor of a singular, passionate voice which is all her own."

—*Financial Times (London)*

ISBN 1-56656-219-8 · $29.95 hb
ISBN 1-56656-254-6 · $12.95 pb · 248 pages

from Jordan

Pillars of Salt

by Fadia Faqir

"A brilliant Jordanian writer."

—*Malcom Bradbury*

"This is a powerful and distinctive piece of writing, melding the recent history of the country with the continuing personal and political oppression of Arab women."

—*The Sunday Times (London)*

ISBN 1-56656-220-1 · $29.95 hb
ISBN 1-56656-253-8 · $12.95 pb · 256 pages

from Palestine

A Lake Beyond the Wind

by Yahya Yakhlif

trans. by M. Jayyusi and C. Tingley

"Sad, detailed and enlightening, this Paelstinian writer's first work to appear in English covers events in the lakeside village of Samakh during the 1948 Arab-Israeli war."

—*Publishers Weekly*

ISBN 1-56656-301-1 · $12.95 pb · 224 pages

from Lebanon

Samarakand

by Amin Maalouf
trans. by Russell Harris

Winner of the Prix des Maisons de la Presse

"[An] accomplished novel by one of the best European voices to have emerged in the last decade."

—*Kirkus Reviews*

"Remarkable... Maalouf has written an extraordinary book."

—*The Independent (London)*

ISBN 1-56656-200-7 · $35.00 hb
ISBN 1-56656-293-7 · $14.95 pb · 312 pages

from Lebanon

The Gardens of Light

by Amin Maalouf
trans. by Dorthy S. Blair

"A compelling tale... the poignant story of a man born before his time... the character of Mani is carefully and warmly drawn..."

—*Times Literary Supplement (London)*

"Maalouf is as eloquent as ever... [He] weaves tapestries of intrigue that illuminate a broader historical moment... Maalouf, in his engaging prose, goes a considerable way towards restoring Mani to us."

—*The Times (London)*

ISBN 1-56656-247-3 · $25.00 hb
ISBN 1-56656-248-4 · $15.00 pb · 272 pages

from Turkey

Cages on Opposite Shores

by Janet Berkok Shami

"The affirmative power of this work is graced with subtlety and simplicity."

—*Publishers Weekly*

Set in Istanbul, this novel tells the story of Meral, a modern-day Turkish woman searching for identity and renewal after leaving her husband of 11 years and realizing for the first time her part-Armenian heritage.

ISBN 1-56656-165-5 · $24.95 hb
ISBN 1-56656-157-4 · $11.95 pb · 256 pages

from Serbia

The Dawning

by Milka Bajic-Poderegin
trans. by Nadja Poderegin

"A tale of human joy and pain which has the power to stir the heart... *The Dawning* is a jewel of a story, with universal resonance."

—*The Ottowa Citizen*

"Remarkable... a moving portrayal of successive generations of Serbian women."

—*The Spectator (London)*

ISBN 1-56656-198-1 · $29.95 hb
ISBN 1-56656-188-4 · $14.95 pb · 384 pages

from Iran

At the Wall of the Almighty

by Farnoosh Moshiri

Is it really possible for a man to forget who he is? To lose every shred of memory? Loony Kamal, the prison guard, is bent on finding out. Our narrator, though, is even more determined to survive. The grim unreality of life inside the prison falls darkly upon us as our hero fights for his life by retreating into a world of stories—or are they memories? Their relationship—with its inhuman brutality and surprising tenderness—lies at the complicated heart of Moshiri's extraordinary debut novel.

ISBN 1-56656-315-1 · $16.00 pb · 512 pages

from Israel

The Days of Miracles and Wonders

An Epic of the New World Disorder

by Simon Louvish

"This is a very important book by an extremely gifted author. It's too good to win the Booker prize, but I'm sure that Simon Louvish doesn't give a damn about that..."

—Literary Review (London)

"If Roth makes you laugh, Louvish will make you clutch your belly in hysterics. He is very funny."

—Daily Telegraph (London)

ISBN 1-56656-316-X · $16.00 pb · 488 pages

from Jordan

Prairies of Fever

by Ibrahim Nasrallah

trans. by May Jayyusi and Jeremy Reed

"A milestone in postmodern Arabic literature; recommended..."

—Library Journal

"[This Work] unambiguously and courageously affirms the creative powers of the mind."

—World Literature Today

ISBN 1-56656-103-5 · $22.95 hb
ISBN 1-56656-106-X · $9.95 pb · 106 pages

from Israel

The Silencer

by Simon Louvish

A brilliant Israel/Palestine thriller.

"Mr. Louvish has enough combustible talent to earn the comparisons with Joseph Heller, Kurt Vonnegut, and Swift that have come his was. The apposite adjective in the long run will most likely be 'Louvish.'"

—New York Times Book Review

ISBN 1-56656-116-7 · $24.95 hb
ISBN 1-56656-108-6 · $10.95 pb · 256 pages

from Egypt

War in the Land of Egypt

by Yusuf al-Qa'id

"This haunting 1975 novel (which was banned in Egypt) is set during the 1973 October War... A chorus of superbly differentiated villager's voices chronicles the inescapable fate of ... Marsi, an Everyman (his very name means 'Egyptian') whose exile from his identity reverberates powerfully throughout this subtle study of injustice... A marvelous piece of work."

—Kirkus Reviews

ISBN 1-56656-227-9 · $12.95 pb · 192 pages

from Palestine

A Balcony Over the Fakihani

by Liyana Badr

trans. by P. Clark with C. Tingley

"An excellent, moving account of the effects of conflict..."

—Journal of Palestine Studies

"These novellas effectively represent war and suffering from the point of view of disenfranchised peoples, both Beirutis and Palestinians. Recommended..."

—Library Journal

ISBN 1-56656-104-3 · $19.95 hb
ISBN 1-56656-107-8 · $9.95 pb · 128 pages

from Lebanon

The Stone of Laughter

by Hoda Barakat

trans. by Sophie Bennett

Winner of the Al-Naqid Award

"This unusual story of Beirut... offers a vividly detailed portrayal of an unfamiliar culture... a gripping story filled with splendidly drawn secondary figures..."

—Kirkus Reviews

ISBN 1-56656-197-3 · $29.95 hb
ISBN 1-56656-190-6 · $12.95 pb · 240 pages

from Yemen

The Hostage

by Zayd Mutee' Dammaj

trans. by M. Jayyusi and C. Tingley

"The cultural anachronism that was the Imamate of Yemen is artfully captured in *The Hostage*... Dammaj's work vibrantly portrays a real Yemen that is still unknown to many Westerners, even as it is once again torn by revolution. Recommended..."

—Library Journal

ISBN 1-56656-146-9 · $24.95 hb
ISBN 1-56656-140-X · $10.95 pb · 168 pages

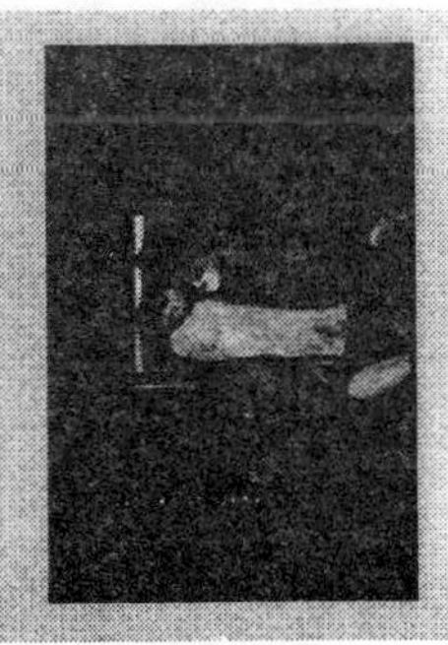

Titles in the

EMERGING VOICES: NEW INTERNATIONAL FICTION

series are available at bookstores everywhere.
To order by phone call toll-free
1–800–238–LINK

⌘

Please have your MasterCard, Visa, or American Express ready when you call. To order by mail, please send your check or money order to the address listed below. For shipping and handling, add $4.00 for the first book and $1.00 for each additional book. Massachusetts residents add 5% sales tax.

⌘

Interlink Publishing Group, Inc.
46 Crosby Street · Northampton, MA 01060
tel (413) 582-7054 · fax (413) 582-7057 · e-mail: interpg@aol.com
website: www.interlinkbooks.com